An Alaskan Gold Mine

The Story of No. 9 Above

An Alaskan Gold Mine

The Story of No. 9 Above

By

Leland H. Carlson

Northwestern University

Introduction
By
Phillip Anderson

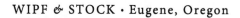

WIPF & STOCK · Eugene, Oregon

Resource Publications
A division of Wipf and Stock Publishers
199 W 8th Ave, Suite 3
Eugene, OR 97401

An Alaskan Gold Mine
The Story of No. 9 Above
By Carlson, Leland
ISBN 13: 978-1-62032-771-5
Publication date 8/1/2015
Previously published by Northwestern University Press, 1951

FOREWORD

A people without interest in its Past is a people without a Future. Undoubtedly many an immigrant from Sweden has been merged in the ocean of American life and contributed something—unconsciously—to his new country. But a richer contribution has been made by those who are aware of the cultural possessions of their father's land and have sought to add something to the character of American life. These have not been content merely to get what they could out of the New World; they have wanted to have a part in creating it.

In 1948 the people of Swedish ancestry in America celebrated in many ways and many places the memory of the pioneers. They resolved to do more than celebrate. They organized an association to preserve the records of the past century and to put into permanent form the story of the migration of a people. They want their children and their grandchildren and their fellow citizens to know the personalities and events which made up the saga of Swedish settlements in America. They hope to give literary expression to a quality of character and to ideals of life which have characterized this historical episode.

Thus the plan of encouraging publications has come into being. The volumes may be of varying length and diverse subject matter. They may tell the story of a pioneer in words of an autobiography, as the Unonius Memoirs do. Or they may describe the strange fortunes of settlements as diverse as New Sweden, Maine, New Sweden, Iowa, or gold digging claims in Alaska. The complete canvas sparkles with names such as Jenny Lind and Fredrika Bremer. It is a fascinating project. Years and funds will be required. But in the end the annals of America will be enriched by the story which the Swedish pioneers have written by their lives, toil, and self-sacrifice.

Vilas Johnson
Nils William Olsson
Conrad Bergendoff

vii

PREFACE

My interest in Alaska began in 1939 when I was writing *A History of North Park College.* It soon became apparent that if I really wished to understand the history of the college and the life of its beloved president, David Nyvall, I would have to study the Alaskan background. It was Alaskan gold from Anvil Creek that made possible the erection of three buildings on the campus; it was Alaskan gold that caused bitter controversy and induced Nyvall to resign the college presidency in 1905. While studying the Alaskan background, I became interested in the subject of gold mining in general and of one gold mine in particular—No. 9 above Discovery claim. I anticipated that the story of No. 9 Above would constitute one chapter; it has become, instead, a book; but the book in turn constitutes only one chapter in the fascinating story of the first great Alaskan stampede to the Seward Peninsula. Few people realize that the Klondike strike was in Canadian territory, and fewer are aware that the discovery of gold at Nome and Anvil Creek was made by Scandinavians.

In the pleasant task of studying the history of gold discoveries in Alaska, and of tracing the story of No. 9 Above, I have incurred many obligations. I am deeply indebted to Mrs. Grace Wickersham and Ruth Coffin, who gave me access to the valuable papers and diaries of Judge James Wickersham. To Edward L. Keithahn, curator of the Alaska Territorial Library and Museum in Juneau, I express my sincere thanks for his aid. In the course of three different visits to Alaska, I obtained help from prospectors, miners, sourdoughs, cheechakoes, merchants, ministers, students, and writers. In visiting thirteen different courts in search of material, I have received courteous treatment from judges, lawyers, clerks of the courts, and vault custodians. I have derived much information from P. H. Anderson, S. G. Cronstedt, Jafet Lindeberg, Carl Lomen, Antonio Polet, and others who were also intimately associated with Nome in the pioneer days of 1898-1901. And I have obtained help from many librarians—especially from Miss Aleene Baker of the Documents Division of Deering Library.

I am grateful to President Theodore W. Anderson, Editor G. F. Hedstrand, Professor E. Gustav Johnson, and Professor Franklin D. Scott, who read the book in manuscript. Carl E. Foyer, August Lundquist, and Eric Haggberg have given expert advice concerning type and format.

I wish to record my gratitude to Dean Theodore C. Blegen of the University of Minnesota, President Conrad Bergendoff of Augustana College, Professor Virgil B. Heltzel, editor of the "Northwestern University Studies," Dr. Nils William Olsson and Mr. Vilas Johnson of the Swedish Pioneer Historical Society.

The Committee on Research of the Graduate School of Northwestern University has generously supported my research. Dean Arthur R. Tebbutt and Professor Gray Boyce have given me sincere interest, genuine encouragement, and tangible aid which cannot be compensated for by a statement in a preface.

Leland H. Carlson

Department of History
Northwestern University

TABLE OF CONTENTS

APPENDICES

LIST OF ILLUSTRATIONS

Introduction to the 2015 Reprint Edition

JAMES A. MICHENER'S MASSIVE novel *Alaska* (1988) recounts in a sweeping yet detailed narrative the history of this vast territory, its native peoples, and those who arrived through time to develop and exploit its natural resources. Chapter Nine, "The Golden Beaches of Nome," is devoted to the pivotal role of Nome in the days of the gold rush at the close of the nineteenth century. Michener located the story first on the astounding discovery of plentiful gold nuggets along the seashore, and then, when those were exhausted, on Anvil Creek, a stream that winds down from the barren hills to the Bering Strait. It is a drama that in particular involves a series of claims numbered from one to nine "above" on the creek, initially "discovered" by three enterprising Swedish immigrants. It includes illegal staking of the claims by others (Norwegians, Lapps, and Siberians), and the subsequent jumping and contesting of ownership of claims five, six, and seven by conniving opportunists aided and abetted by corrupt lawyers and judges in the absence of any established, enforced law. Nome, for centuries a tiny native village, overnight had become in 1899 the largest city in Alaska with 30,000 mostly poor and greedy male prospectors—with everything, vices included, that accompanied a boom town. In the previous year, Nome and its environs had yielded $7.5 million in gold (valued at twenty dollars an ounce at the time), slightly more than the much ballyhooed purchase of Seward's Folly in 1867. "But you had to be on the scene," Michener wrote, "to appreciate the real insanity of life in Alaska, and no better laboratory for analysis than Nome could have been found" (p. 478).

Michener does not fully document the sources researched for the content of his story, but described in general what is fact-based and what is fiction. In addition to historical documents, they surely included in terms of ethos a bestselling novel of 1906 entitled *The Spoilers* by

Rex Beach. It is a thriller contemporary with the gold rush in Nome. All the essential historical characters and details are in place, notably in thinly disguised pseudonyms the shady North Dakota politician, Alexander McKenzie; his legal lackey, U.S. District Judge Arthur M. Noyes; and the ruthless prospector, Paddy Ryan (not the boxer). Together they stole millions until President Theodore Roosevelt removed Noyes in 1902. The book, of course, made fictional romance and unrequited love central to the plot. Soon made into a play, Hollywood film versions followed in 1914, 1923, 1930 (with Gary Cooper), 1942 (with Marlene Dietrich, Randolph Scott, and John Wayne), and 1955 (with Anne Baxter, Jeff Chandler, and Rory Calhoun). One can only wonder where the publicized "Rex Beach's Tremendous Adventure!" found its historical origins as "a true story."

I first read Leland Carlson's *An Alaskan Gold Mine: The Story of No. 9 Above* more than thirty years ago, before the appearance of Michener's novel or ever hearing of Rex Beach. My immediate impression was that this should be made into a movie! Yes, the romance was absent, but the compelling ingredients were there: Swedish immigrant missionaries consumed by gold fever, staking claims in areas shown to them by native friends and having them jumped by murky and notorious opportunists; the youngest and most recent arrival cashing in hugely on a claim initially staked in the name of a young Eskimo boy; a financially strapped Swedish-American denomination in Chicago, aided by older jealous missionaries, contesting ownership and inaugurating more than two decades of legal battles winding their way to the Supreme Court of the United States; allegations of sexual misconduct and payoffs; exploitation of native Alaskans, a sad saga of gold, greed, and grief where no one was spared damage to personal reputation and well-being; a church leader and college president resigning and entering voluntary exile; and finally what Carlson concluded to be a story that "resembles the fable of the person who killed the goose that laid the golden eggs." Most of the money, calculated in today's dollars as roughly 9.6 million, ended up in the pockets of lawyers. While only one of the hundreds of legal suits that occurred over many years where claims and mining rights were contested, Number 9 Above is arguably the most protracted and famous for its many dimensions and great wealth.

The story does indeed begin in 1898 with Three Lucky Swedes, whose fame is still kept alive in books and television documentaries in

Sweden, together having formed the Pioneer Mining Company. John Brynteson, a coal miner from Michigan, was joined by Eric O. Lindblom, a tailor and sailor from San Francisco. The third, Jafet Lindeberg, was not even Swedish but was a Norwegian reindeer herder, lured to Alaska by the ambitious plans of the Presbyterian missionary educator, Sheldon Jackson, to provide economic opportunity and security for native villages. What then unfolded involved not only the usual legal technicalities but the much more intriguing nexus of personalities, the machinations of an immigrant denominational leadership thousands of miles away in Chicago, and the tragic ethical shortcomings of otherwise good and decent people. The central character is Peter H. Anderson, a young graduate of North Park College, the seminary of the Swedish Evangelical Mission Covenant Church, located in Chicago. In the summer of 1897 he was assigned to teach Eskimo children at the mission station in the village of Golovin on the Seward Peninsula. In 1895 it had included three missionaries, one native assistant, forty-nine pupils, and about thirty "converted" natives in attendance at weekly worship services.

After the Three Lucky Swedes staked nine claims and assigned ownership on Anvil Creek, they returned to Golovin and sought the advice of a veteran miner, Gabriel Price. There were two major problems: first, the claims were not legal because the dimensions were wrong and needed to be re-staked; and second, claims eight and nine were in the names of young Eskimos, Constantine Uparazuck and Gabriel Adams, legally underage and, more importantly, U.S. law prohibited natives from owning claims. According to the 1867 Treaty of Cession with Russia, Eskimos were classified with foreigners as "aliens," and they were not granted citizenship until 1924 by an act of Congress. Number 8 was then reassigned to Gabriel Price, who did very well with the claim, and Number 9 to P. H. Anderson, who paid Price twenty dollars but was listed as a "trustee." And herein was the source of legal battles to come: was Anderson a trustee for the Eskimo boys, the mission station at Golovin, the Covenant Church, or all parties? Number 9 Above was named the "Mission Claim" by Anderson, but he qualified that by saying it was because it was never worked on Sundays. With all this ambiguity, who in fact owned the mine?

The Mission Claim immediately began to yield abundant gold. Meanwhile, a group of Covenant leaders in Chicago had formed the

Good Hope Mining Company, speculating (at least 4,500 claims were made in the Seward Peninsula, and most of its claims staked by Brynteson proved worthless) while at the same time watching Number 9 Above closely and eagerly. Taking out $50,000 ($1.47M today) the first year in 1899, the $10,000 ($294,000 today) that Anderson offered the denomination was considered "a mere trifle." Twenty percent was not enough; the church wanted more. Though offended and withholding the payment, Anderson nevertheless indicated his willingness to remain generous in his gifts. An additional $175,000 ($5.09M today) of gold emerged from the mine in 1900, and Anderson wrote in February 1901 that he would gift $54,000 ($1.55M today) to North Park and the Covenant hospital if he received a signed release. The Covenant executive board replied by asking for $100,000 plus half of all future proceeds to grant the release.

Leland Carlson meticulously recounts how matters devolved further from there. Anderson refused, and the executive board eventually did sign the release and received the $54,000 (North Park University has two buildings on campus built with Alaska gold), but then reneged on its formal agreement when an older missionary, Nels Hultberg, convinced leaders that he could prove that the Covenant Church owned the mine. He struck a deal where he would work the mine on behalf of the church for half its proceeds. Together, law suits were filed that seesawed through the system with various rulings. Carlson sees Hultberg as the villain in the saga, the Covenant's aging president, Carl August Björk, as in over his head, and David Nyvall (president of North Park and the denomination's secretary, who handled all the correspondence) as a victim of collateral damage. Accused of sexual assault by the family of an Eskimo girl, Dora Adams, Anderson settled out of court for $15,000 ($416,000 today); he also agreed to satisfy the prior claims of the two Eskimo boys by promising $57,000 ($1.58M today) to their families, but this was never paid. Nyvall, who signed the release only to see the minutes struck from the record by others, was angered and ethically offended. He alone defended Anderson's rightful ownership based on the evidence, despite the allegations of immoral behavior (which he did not defend one way or the other, seeing them as irrelevant to the legal issue of ownership), and he paid a huge price (resignation from North Park in 1904 and a hiatus away from Chicago until 1912), a stand ultimately upheld by the Supreme Court.

While the Three Lucky Swedes who became incredibly wealthy are still remembered in their native homeland (Brynteson is known as the Gold King), Alaskan natives on the Seward Peninsula keep alive the memories of Constantine and Gabriel (both of whom died tragically young), as well as those who helped the foreigners "discover" the gold in the first place. To a story of "gold, greed, and grief," today must be added the reality of "grab." Previously muted or ignored, this injustice is of contemporary importance. It also set back for generations whatever altruistic mission work, then only a decade old, was being done by Covenanters in Alaska.

This brief sketch of events whets the appetite for the engaging read of *An Alaskan Gold Mine*. It is an intertwined narrative of turn-of-the-century native culture and exploitation in Alaska; the evangelistic desires of an immigrant church and its missionary activity; the testing of ecclesial polity and exercise of powerful personalities; the influential role of highly vocal newspapers and their ability to sway public opinion—often through rumor and innuendo—like a soap opera played out week by week; the American legal system with all its flaws and snail-paced (and expensive) procedures; and the golden glitter of money—whether for personal gain or advancing the Kingdom of God.

Leland Henry Carlson (1908-1995), born to Swedish immigrant parents in Rockford, Illinois, was an eminent historian of sixteenth- and seventeenth-century British history, particularly the dissenting tradition of Elizabethan and early Stuart Puritanism. Raised in the Swedish Mission Covenant Church, Carlson was a graduate of Beloit College (B.A. 1931), Chicago Theological Seminary (B.D. 1938), and the University of Chicago (Ph.D. 1939). He joined the faculty of North Park College in 1936, becoming head of the social science division, as well as dean of men. While at North Park Carlson published the fiftieth anniversary history of the school, *History of North Park College* (1941), and became close friends with the school's founding president, David Nyvall (1863-1946), whom he deeply admired. He soon became academically interested in Number 9 Above, not only because it appealed to his detective-like research methods but as a means of vindicating his beloved Nyvall by setting the record straight in a truthful account based on thousands of sources. For more than a decade, Carlson made yearly visits to Alaska unearthing records and interviewing eye witnesses. He meticulously compiled every court record and transcripts of depositions. He explored church minutes and a mountain of newspaper coverage in the ethnic press. This is a history that need not be written again.

Carlson left for Northwestern University in 1942, where he was an award-winning teacher and increasingly prolific scholar. His administrative abilities were also recognized, and in 1954 he accepted the presidency of Rockford College where he remained for five years. He then taught at the Southern California School of Theology in Claremont, and in retirement was a scholar in residence at the Huntington Library in nearby San Marino. A *festschrift* was presented to him in 1975: *The Dissenting Tradition: Essays for Leland H. Carlson*, eds., C. Robert Cole and Michael E. Moody (Athens: Ohio University Press). It contains a substantive biographical essay and tribute by Franklin D. Scott, Carlson's colleague and friend at both Northwestern University and the Huntington Library.

There is an interesting backstory to the publishing of *An Alaskan Gold Mine*, revealing that the wounds had barely healed, even after a half-century. Published by Northwestern University Press in 1951, it was actually scheduled to appear a year earlier as the first publication of the Swedish Pioneer Historical Society, recently formed in Chicago in 1948. This followed a year-long celebration throughout the United States of a centennial observance (the plans to celebrate in 1941 were interrupted by the war) of the beginnings of the mass migration of 1.3 million Swedes to America. The events culminated in June 1948 at Chicago Stadium, attended by more than 16,000 Swedish Americans. Addresses were given by Prince Bertil of Sweden, President Harry Truman, and the poet Carl Sandburg (who became honorary chair of the Society). Re-named the Swedish-American Historical Society in 1982, it continues to publish a quarterly journal and scholarly books in the field of immigration and ethnicity. Two of its enthusiastic founders were Algoth Ohlson, president of North Park, and Theodore W. Anderson, president of the Covenant Church. They urged Carlson and the Society's board of directors, however, to publish the book elsewhere, fearing the renewed festering of the controversy, not based on the facts—which they welcomed—but upon layers of church politics, memory, and prejudice. Carlson understood and graciously acceded to the request.

The original Northwestern University Press publication has been exceedingly difficult to acquire. While it took me fifteen years to find a copy, gratefully there is now ready access to this dramatic story and its intriguing characters, thanks to Wipf and Stock. Its fascination is enduring and its lessons are timeless.

Philip J. Anderson, D.Phil.
Professor Emeritus of Church History
North Park Theological Seminary
President
Swedish-American Historical Society

PART I—1898-1901

BACKGROUND AND BEGINNINGS
OF CONFLICT

BACKGROUND AND BEGINNINGS

EIGHTY YEARS AGO, in 1867, the United States purchased Alaska from Russia at a cost of $7,200,000. Little did people realize then how significant "Seward's icebox" would become. Yet, within the short span of four score years Alaska has become a part of the daily life of Americans. Alaska's salmon is found on the tables of poor and rich, Alaskan gold has enriched our mints, furs from the far north can be seen on Michigan Boulevard or Fifth Avenue, and books about Alaskan life have become an accepted part of American literature. Even more significant, Alaska has become a connecting link between Asia and North America; and the landing fields of Nome, Anchorage, Juneau, and Ketchikan are centers of bustling daily traffic. Because of her strategic location, Alaska is becoming one of the great bastions of defense for the entire western hemisphere.

Aside from the wider implications of our purchase of Alaska, we may note how Alaska has lured thousands of adventurers, miners, merchants, prospectors, and tourists to her shores. Just fifty years ago a steamer arrived in Seattle "with a ton of gold." [1] As the news spread, men flocked to the new diggings in the Klondike and along the Yukon. Dangerous Chilkoot passes, hostile Indians, precipitous dead-horse gulches, perilous rapids, as well as cold, ice, loneliness and starvation, were unable to stem that powerful tide of humanity that surged into the new land.

As the search for gold widened, men penetrated into the barren tundra fields of the Seward Peninsula. The discovery of gold at Council City, Ophir Creek, Anvil Creek, Sinuk River, and Candle [2] led to a new stampede that reached its climax in

[1] The steamer *S. S. Portland* arrived on July 17, 1897.
[2] Council City is about forty miles north of Golovnin Bay, at the junction of the Niukluk River and Melsing Creek. Four miles to the west is Ophir Creek. Anvil Creek is a tributary of Snake River, near Nome. Fifteen miles to the west of Nome is the Sinuk River. Candle is on the Kiwalik River in the northwest corner of the Seward Peninsula.

1900 when approximately 18,000 people were dumped on the shores of Nome within a space of seven weeks.

Little did men dream that what was happening in the Seward Peninsula would have ramifications throughout the United States. And even less did people within the Evangelical Mission Covenant Church of America realize that what was transpiring at Cheenik and Cape Nome would alter the course of events in San Francisco, Chicago and Washington, D. C.

The Discovery of Gold at Nome—1898

The story of No. 9 Above is one connecting link between Alaska and Chicago. From this gold mine came the money that made possible the erection of two buildings on the campus of North Park College.[3] From this mine came donations which made possible the building of the Swedish Covenant Hospital. And from the glittering gold found on bed-rock came deep-seated hatreds, bitter recriminations, headaches for committee members and heartaches for two Covenant presidents, as well as eighteen years of litigation that involved eleven different courts and reached the U. S. Supreme Court four times. To understand this litigation, we need to know the story of the discovery of gold at Nome and the chief persons who played roles therein.

In 1894 a young man came to Chicago to continue his education. His name was Peter H. Anderson, and he came from a farm near Des Moines, Iowa. Enrolling in the Academy of North Park College, he studied two years with the purpose of becoming a minister of the gospel, but he was encouraged by the school officials to prepare for the work of a missionary instead. Accordingly, he spent the third school year, 1896-1897, in a program combining academic study with practical work at the Covenant Home of Mercy, a small hospital under the direction of Dr. Claes W. Johnson. After acquiring the rudiments of a medical education, Anderson sailed from San

---

[3] These are Wilson Hall, built originally as a boys' dormitory, and the old Music School, used first as the home of President David Nyvall. The gymnasium was made possible by a donation of $15,000 from John Brynteson, who obtained his money from Alaska's gold also, especially from No. 1 Above on Anvil Creek.

4

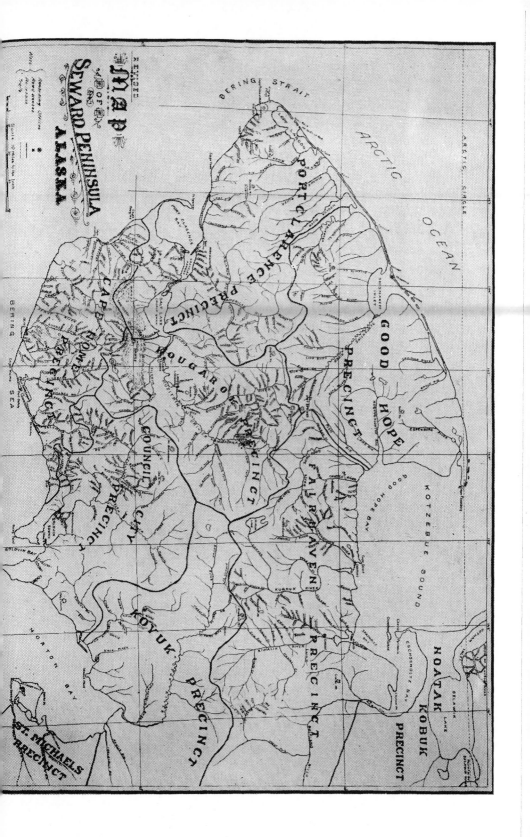

Mining on No. 9 Above, Anvil Creek, about four miles north of Nome, Alaska, in 1900. S. G. Cronstedt (fourth from the left) has kindly supplied me with these pictures. Note the tundra, tents, and mountains in the background. Note also the sluice boxes, hose, and tailings.

Francisco aboard the *Volant* on June 9, 1897, for northern Alaska.[4]

Ten years earlier the Evangelical Mission Covenant Church of America had sent its first missionary, A. E. Karlson, to Unalakleet, on Norton Sound. Then in 1893 a second missionary, Nels O. Hultberg, established a station at Cheenik on Golovnin Bay.[5] This was a barren spot, near a small Eskimo village, with only one white inhabitant, John A. Dexter, who had established a small trading post. It was at this station that Anderson arrived on August 12, 1897, to serve as a school-teacher for the Eskimos.

Whereas Anderson came to Alaska to serve the cause of God, thousands of Americans and Canadians were hurrying into the country to prospect for gold. The rush to the Klondike was increasing. Some intrepid adventurers, seeking to circumvent the difficult passage over the Chilkoot Pass, came to St. Michael, assembled their boats, and proceeded up the Yukon River to Dawson City.

Among those infected with the gold fever was missionary Hultberg. With a miner, George Johanson, he had prospected the Seward Peninsula for gold as early as 1895, and since then had continued his prospecting trips.[6] He was convinced from reports of Dexter the trader and of natives that gold was to be found in the vicinity. Naturally, he was not a little excited when a party of four men from San Francisco—H. L. Blake, D. B. Libby, L. F. Melsing, and A. P. Mordaunt—arrived at Cheenik on September 17, 1897, in search of gold. This party proceeded up the Fish River, established camp about forty miles inland, and named the place Council City.[7] These men were unable to carry on mining operations during the

[4] Sheldon Jackson, *Report on Introduction of Domestic Reindeer into Alaska*, 55th Congress, 2nd session (serial 3590), Senate Document No. 30 (1898), p. 80.

[5] Theodor Anderson, *Svenska Missionsförbundet, dess uppkomst and femtioåriga verksamhet* (Stockholm, 1928), pp. 12, 37-39; *Årsberättelse från Svenska Evangeliska Missions-Förbundets i Amerika nionde verksamhetsår* (1893), p. 20.

[6] George Johanson came to Alaska in 1894, on the same boat that brought Mrs. Hultberg. He was the first discoverer of gold in the Council City area, about forty miles north of Golovnin Bay.

[7] H. L. Blake, "History of the Discovery of Gold at Cape Nome," 56 Congress, 1st session (serial 3878), Senate Document No. 441 (1900), p. 2.

winter, but they did make prospecting trips. Guided by Hultberg, Blake proceeded to Cape Nome in January, 1898, and with the same guide, Libby went as far as Port Clarence in the spring.[8]

About April 21, 1898, Anderson and Hultberg, accompanied by John Tornensis, a Lapp reindeer herder, went to Council City. On April 24 and 25, these men staked claims on Melsing Creek and Ophir Creek. Having joined with the other four men in organizing the first mining district in northern Alaska, the men recorded their claims. Hultberg's claims were No. 5 on Melsing Creek and No. 6 on Ophir Creek; Anderson's claims were No. 6 on Melsing and No. 7 on Ophir Creek.

After the staking and recording, Anderson returned to Cheenik, but Hultberg set out on a long exploring trip. After a month's absence, he arrived home at Cheenik about May 18, returned to Council City about May 21 to help A. E. Karlson, Edwin Engelstad, and Dr. A. N. Kittilsen stake claims. During June and July he made three more trips to Council City and conducted at least seven prospectors to the new diggings.[9]

During July there arrived at the Cheenik station three men destined to become significant in the story of Nome's gold mines. John Brynteson and John L. Hagelin arrived together on July 21. Brynteson had been a coal miner in Michigan. Having decided to look for gold instead of mining coal, he set out for Alaska in June. Hagelin accompanied him as the agent of a group of Covenant men who had formed the Good Hope Mining Co.[10] About July 22 there arrived at the station a small, bewhiskered, famished man—Eric O. Lindblom. He had been a tailor in San Francisco, where he contracted the gold fever. Without funds and without an adequate knowledge of English, he unwittingly signed up for two years with the

8 Supreme Court of the State of Illinois, No. 7712, Record to Supreme Court, pp. 1466, 1469, 1475, 1477 f. This typescript consists of 2667 pages of valuable material, and is filed in the office of the clerk of the court at Springfield, Illinois. Hereafter referred to as MS. Record.

9 Ibid., pp. 1475-1481. These seven prospectors probably came to Golovnin Bay about June 15-20—as soon after the ice-breakup as possible.

10 The Good Hope Mining Co. was incorporated July 5, 1899, by Claes Flodin, C. August Youngquist, and Hjalmar J. Lind. Others elected were O. P. Anderson, C. A. Bjork, E. J. Bjorkross, and Aaron Carlson (From a letter of the Secretary of State, Edward J. Barrett). The company probably was informally organized in the spring of 1898, since it sent John Hagelin to Alaska in June, 1898.

crew of a whaling ship, sailed to Port Clarence, and there jumped ship about July 5.[11] Proceeding eastward about one hundred forty miles along the shores of the Seward Peninsula, he managed to reach Cheenik. To provide for his wants and to satisfy his lust for gold, Hultberg grub-staked him to work on his claims in the Council City mining district.

While Lindblom was proceeding to Council City, Hultberg and Blake made plans for a second trip to Cape Nome. Hultberg invited Brynteson and Hagelin to accompany him; Blake invited H. L. Porter and Chris Kimber to join the group. Setting out on July 31, the party reached Snake River and Nome on August 4. The following day the men prospected the creeks of the region. Hultberg found excellent prospects on Anvil Creek, but did his best to conceal the fact, and he persuaded Blake to continue westward toward Sinuk River. At this point, Blake and Hultberg parted company; Blake went up the river to prospect and Hultberg returned to Cheenik, arriving about August 16, followed about a week later by Brynteson and Hagelin. No claims were staked on this trip, but Hultberg was convinced that the prospects were very good.[12]

Since Hultberg had been in Alaska for five years, he had decided to return to the United States. Before leaving, however, he encouraged Brynteson and Hagelin to return, and he urged Lindblom to accompany them. On August 31 he left for the States, just three weeks before one of the greatest gold strikes in American history—a discovery for which he had been largely responsible.

Hardly had Hultberg departed when Brynteson, Lindblom and Jafet Lindeberg[13] left Council City, on September 6, for

[11] Arvid Höijer and Georg af Forselles, *Svenska Greven av Alaska. Guldgrävarliv i Nome, Candle, och Fairbanks* (Stockholm, 1934), pp. 51-58. See also E. S. Harrison, *Nome and Seward Peninsula* (Seattle, 1905), p. 202.

[12] For the story of these two trips, see Leland H. Carlson, "The Discovery of Gold at Nome, Alaska," *The Pacific Historical Review*, September, 1946, pp. 261-266; "The First Mining Season at Nome, Alaska—1899," *Ibid.*, May, 1947, pp. 163-175. See further Leland H. Carlson, "Nome: From Mining Camp to Civilized Community," *Pacific Northwest Quarterly*, July, 1947, pp. 233-242.

[13] Lindeberg was a young Norwegian, who came to the U. S. in 1898 with a party of reindeer herders hired by Sheldon Jackson, a government agent of the Department of the Interior. Sheldon Jackson, *Ninth Annual Report on the Introduction of Domestic Reindeer into Alaska* (1900), 56th Congress, 1st session, (serial 3928), House Document No. 5, p. 1404.

Cheenik. At the mission station Anderson was now in charge. He encouraged the trio in their plan to return to Nome, and sold them supplies from the station for the trip.

The three men set out on September 11 and arrived in Nome September 15. After spending a week prospecting and locating claims on Glacier Creek, Snow Gulch, and Mountain Creek, they staked on September 22 the rich claims on Anvil Creek. Discovery claim was staked jointly. No. 1 Below was staked for Lindeberg, No. 1 Above for Brynteson, and No. 6 Above for Lindblom. In addition to these four claims, there were seven more claims staked by powers of attorney. Brynteson staked No. 3 Below for Dr. J. R. Gregory, No. 2 Above for P. H. Anderson, No. 3 Above for John L. Hagelin, No. 4 Above for A. E. Karlson and No. 5 Above for Nels O. Hultberg. Lindeberg staked No. 2 Below for W. A. Kjellman and No. 4 Below for John A. Dexter.[14]

Besides these eleven claims, there is some slight evidence that No. 7 Above was staked by a power of attorney for Dr. A. N. Kittilsen. No. 8 Above seems to have been intended for Constantine, an Eskimo lad, and No. 9 Above for another young Eskimo, Gabriel. After a week of staking and prospecting, the miners returned to Cheenik on October 2 with about $50 in sample gold dust.

While these men had been prospecting, Anderson had gone to St. Michael. There he met Gabriel W. Price, who had just come from the Kotzebue Sound region where he had been unsuccessful in finding prospects of gold. Encouraged to try the Council City region, Price returned with Anderson to Cheenik. Here he met Brynteson, Lindblom, and Lindeberg, who announced their discoveries but refused to divulge the location of their claims. In talking with Price, who was an experienced miner, the Scandinavians became apprehensive about the legality of their holdings. They had staked their claims with two stakes instead of six; they had laid out their claims to be 1500 x 600 feet, whereas the correct dimensions should have been 1320 x 660. Furthermore, they had not organized a

14 Gregory was a government doctor at St. Michael; Kjellman was a superintendent of reindeer; Dexter was a trader married to an Eskimo and living at Cheenik.

mining district and they had not recorded their claims. If No. 8 and No. 9 had been staked for the Eskimos, there was the legal question of their citizenship and of their being under twenty-one years of age.[15]

In these circumstances the miners decided to return to Nome and restake their claims. One suggestion made was that the party should travel to Nome by reindeer as soon as snowfall would permit. Another suggestion was that the party should use a large Eskimo umiak. But a solution was reached when Anderson agreed to allow the use of the mission station's four-ton, two-masted schooner on condition that the miners help him build a schoolhouse. The bargain was made, the schoolhouse was built, and the schooner was loaded with food and equipment. In order to have six men for the organization of a mining district, the three miners invited Dr. A. N. Kittilsen,[16] Price, and John Tornensis to accompany them. Constantine, the Eskimo boy, who knew how to sail the schooner, also was included.

Setting sail on October 12, the party arrived at Snake River on October 15, organized that same day the Cape Nome Mining District, and adopted a set of laws and rules. Thereupon they restaked their claims and shortened them from 1,500 feet to 1,320 feet. Then they recorded their claims with Dr. Kittilsen, the newly elected District Recorder. Since Discovery Claim was shortened 180 feet on the upper end, it was necessary to shorten No. 1 Above 360 feet, No. 2 Above 540 feet, No. 3 Above 720 feet, No. 4 Above 900 feet, No. 5 Above 1,080 feet, and No. 6 Above 1,260 feet. This alteration affected Lindblom particularly, who had selected No. 6 Above originally, and who now found that the new No. 6 Above was on the ground of the old No. 5 Above, with the exception of the upper sixty feet. If any claims had been staked beyond

---

[15] Legally, Eskimos could hold claims, but in actual practice, their illiteracy and inability to cope with jumpers left them helpless. Only the U. S. Government could challenge an Eskimo claim. See *Nels O. Hulberg* v. *Frideborg A. Anderson,* United States Circuit Court of Appeals, Eighth Circuit, No. 4837, *Petition for Rehearing by Appellee,* p. 41. See also MS. Record, p. 1583.

[16] Dr. Kittilsen was a government physician and a reindeer superintendent, first stationed at Port Clarence and then at Eaton Reindeer Station near Unalakleet.

No. 6 Above, they were also affected. Dr. Kittilsen staked No. 7 Above for himself, Price staked No. 8 Above for himself and No. 9 Above for his brother, R. L. Price, by a power of attorney.

By the first week in November the party found it necessary to discontinue work. They had managed to stake claims on several creeks, and in five days with two rockers had obtained $1,800. But ice had formed in the creeks, and it had become too cumbersome to soften the earth by fires. Setting out with a native and dog team, they encountered Anderson and Magnus Kjelsberg [17] on the trail with reindeer and sleds. With great exhilaration of spirit the miners recounted their experiences and proudly displayed their gold. Triumphantly the party returned to Cheenik about November 15.

Two days later, G. W. Price legally conveyed No. 9 Above to Anderson for a consideration of $20. This transfer had been prearranged, but the reasons for this previous agreement are difficult to ascertain. According to Price and Anderson, the reason for the agreement was that Anderson had conferred a favor on Price by transporting him from St. Michael to Cheenik and by making it possible for Price to investigate the gold fields at Council City and Nome. When Price set out for Nome, Anderson requested Price, whom he knew to be an experienced miner, to stake a claim near where he staked for himself; Price agreed to this request and kept his promise.

According to those who disagreed with this interpretation, No. 8 and No. 9 Above were originally intended for the Eskimo boys. Since it was believed that the Eskimo boys could not legally own claims, the miners decided to give No. 8 Above to Price and No. 9 Above to Anderson *as a trustee*. This contention of the existence of a trusteeship was the beginning of misunderstandings and ugly rumors and sharp disagreements. These in turn led to litigation that lasted until 1919, involved some of the keenest legal minds in the country, and divided public opinion into two great camps.

The opponents of Anderson agree on the existence of a

[17] Kjelsberg came from Kaafjord, Norway, to the United States in 1898 to drive reindeer cross country for the relief of destitute miners on the Yukon River.

trusteeship, but disagree on the beneficiaries of this arrangement. It is contended that Anderson was a trustee for the Eskimo boys personally, or for the mission station, or for the Eskimo boys and the mission station jointly, or for the denomination which paid his expenses. Anderson's opponents further agree that he was the only one to possess two claims on Anvil Creek. This argument needs to be counterbalanced with the facts that Anderson supplied the schooner and part of the provisions, that he met the party with reindeer and sleds, that he had done Price a signal favor, and that whereas he had two claims on Anvil Creek, others in the party held anywhere from five to thirty claims on various creeks in the Cape Nome Mining District.[18]

The First Mining Season of 1899

During the winter months of 1898-99 it was impossible to carry on mining operations. But the cold weather did not deter men at Council City and St. Michael and on the Kobuk River from stampeding to the new diggings. By dog-team and reindeer, men hurried to the new Eldorado to stake claims.[19] Among those who feverishly followed their sleds to Nome was Lindblom, the impoverished forlorn tailor from San Francisco, returning in the dead of winter to the region which had transformed him into a wealthy grasping miner obsessed with the idea of gobbling up as many claims as possible.[20]

Something of the spirit of the times, and something of the activities of the last three months of 1898, can be obtained from the letter which Anderson wrote at this time:

[18] Brynteson had at least five claims, Lindeberg eight, and Lindblom thirty (*Congressional Record, Senate,* April 30, 1900, p. 4841). These three men formed The Pioneer Mining Company, and in their corporate capacity held additional property.

[19] It is truly amazing how quickly the news spread throughout northern Alaska. By February, 1899, the news had been carried almost the entire length of the Yukon River (*Yukon Press, Circle, Alaska,* February 15, 1899, p. 1).

[20] Fred R. Cowden, "Cape Nome Mining District," *The Alaska Pioneer,* June 13, 1913, pp. 4-12. This article supplies detailed and accurate data.

Golovin Bay, Alaska
January 1, 1899

Mr. N. O. Hultberg
Chicago, Illinois.

My Dear Friend:

You must excuse me for not writing you long before, but knowing that you were to take a trip to Sweden you would not get my letter before you came back to Chicago. Now, as mail leaves St. Michael once a month, I hope this will reach you while in Chicago. I am feeling fairly well now, but I have been sick ever since the cold weather set in, and I feel I cannot stand the winters up here. I have written the Board to send some one here in my place next summer.

You will never be forgotten in that you asked me to send some one up to Cape Nome to investigate the country you had been in but so short a time that you did not find the hidden treasure, but you thought it was there, and when Brynteson, Lindblom, Linderberg had prospected the country they found very good prospects. They brought back about $50. But as there was no district organized we all thought it best for them to return and organize so as to record the claims. Dr. Kittelsen, Johan and Mr. Price, a California miner, went with them. I let them have the schooner so that they could bring all they needed. The schooner is to be there until the ice goes out. Well, these men worked up there with two rockers for about five days after they had gotten everything ready. And the result of their labor was a great surprise to them, as for all who hear it. They washed out nearly $1,800. One day they cleaned up over $600. The best pan they got was $8.41. Most of the gold was taken from what was called Anvil Creek Claim Nos. 7 and 8. Yours is No. 5 and mine is 2 Above. But our claims are jumped. Mr. Mordaunt has jumped yours, and there is a French doctor in Council City has jumped mine. Mr. Haglin's also is jumped and also Kjelberg. Mr. Carlson's was also jumped, but was not recorded. The others are recorded for the second time. The reason they give for jumping is, they say, powers of attorneys are not legal. But I think we will hold our claims.

12

This new find has caused great excitement; everyone, both from Council City as well as from St. Michael, that could get there went. I never seen such excitement before. I have heard several miners say they think this is going to beat Klondyke, and it must be rich when it averages $1 to a pan on the surface. You better come as early as you can to look after your interests. Hoping you are enjoying yourself well, with many regards to you and your better half, I remain,

Your friend,

P. H. Anderson.

P. S. Three hundred claims are recorded in the Cape Nome Mining District now and many more are located. Dr. Kittelsen is recorder.[21]

By January, 1899, more than 300 claims had been legally recorded and more had been staked. Such rapid and indiscriminate staking inevitably led to trouble. Some of the best claims were "jumped" by those malcontents who took what they wanted without being bothered by qualms of conscience. Among the claims jumped were the missionary claims—those of Karlson, Hultberg, and Anderson. Since there were no courts, troops or commissioners at Nome, the issues were held in abeyance until L. B. Shephard, U. S. Commissioner from St. Michael, held a special court session at Cheenik on March 20-23, 1899. In all cases on the docket, Shephard decided in favor of the original stakers, denounced the jumpers, and sent one of them to jail at St. Michael.[22]

By July of 1899, Nome jumped from a population of 250 to 2,500. Among the new arrivals was Hultberg, who made preparations for his claim No. 5. Anderson was also present, having brought supplies from Cheenik to Nome in the course of the long winter. Hardly had Anderson begun operations on No. 9 Above before it was jumped. The jumper was Paddy Ryan, a notorious character among the miners and a prize

[21] MS. Record, p. 1524.

[22] See the letter of Lieutenant Oliver Spaulding, April 13, 1899, to the Adjutant, Fort St. Michael; National Archives, War Department Records, Department of the Columbia 1743. See also letter of Captain E. S. Walker, May 2, 1899, *ibid*. See further 56 Congress, 1st session (serial 3868), Senate Document No. 272. p. 13.

fighter of no mean ability.[23] Despite warnings from the lieutenant of a U. S. Army Detachment, Ryan refused to abandon his jumper's title and had to be forced off the claim. Thereafter Anderson's mining operations continued throughout the summer months and by the fall he had extracted from the mine approximately $50,000.

When Anderson returned in the fall to Seattle, he was a rich man. He had decided to give up his work as a teacher in Alaska, and he had determined to reside in the States. Frideborg A. Erickson, whom he had known as a nurse at the Covenant Home of Mercy, was his fiancée, and on November 20, 1899, they were married. Shortly prior to his marriage, he promised to give her the proceeds of No. 2 Above, and on December 26, 1899, he gave her the Hafner farm of 960 acres in Dickinson County, Kansas.[24]

The Background of the Controversy

By the fall of 1899 the first mining season had ended, and as a result several developments had come into clearer focus. One was the obvious fact that No. 2 Above was a poor claim and that No. 9 Above was a rich claim. Another was the growing resentment and jealousy of Hultberg. As one of the pioneers, he felt that he deserved better from those whom he had aided in becoming wealthy. Instead, he had been dogged by hard luck. He had left Alaska just three weeks before one of the most momentous gold strikes in the entire territory. When he returned to Nome in June, 1899, he had been one of the first victims of typhoid fever. His own mines were considered good paying property, but because of poor management were not yielding their optimum values.

23 Some idea of the character of this man may be gathered from the following story. At a scheduled boxing match at Nome, one of the contestants failed to appear. The other fighter announced, to the delight of the crowd, that he was willing to fight any man in the house, but there was "wan dirty dog" he would like to lay his hands on. Was Paddy Ryan in the house? If so, would he dare to show his cowardly length? Paddy was present, charged into the ring, and fought like an animal. Both men went down in a double knockout (Rex Beach, *Personal Exposures* [N. Y.: Harper Bros., 1940], p. 89).

24 United States Circuit Court of Appeals, Eight Circuit, No. 4837; *Frideborg A. Anderson* vs. *Nels O. Hultberg, Transcript of Record*, pp. 252 f. Hereafter referred to as *Transcript of Record, No. 4837*. These records are in the office of the clerk of the court at St. Louis, Missouri.

The most significant development was the deepening rivalry between Anderson and Hultberg. Ever since the arrival of Anderson at Golovnin Bay in 1897, there had been a lack of rapport because of the different temperaments of the two men. Hultberg was an adventurous, rough type of man, with a background of blacksmithing and mechanical work, ever optimistic, visionary, open and aggressive. Lacking formal education, he probably was secretly envious of and mildly doubtful of Anderson who was more realistic, practical, cautious and reserved. When the two men had staked claims on Ophir and Melsing creeks in the Council City region, Hultberg began to make statements of what he would do with his gold before it was panned and promised to give two-thirds of what he got to the Covenant, but Anderson would "not promise anything of that kind." When Hultberg grub-staked Eric Lindblom and John Watterson to work these mines, he included Anderson's mines without consulting the owner.[25]

During the summer of 1899, Hultberg sought to elicit from Anderson something of his plans for No. 9 Above. Hultberg regarded Anderson as a trustee or as a manager for the mine, and he urged Anderson not to pay himself more than $15 a day for superintending the claim. Since this was the Mission Claim, argued Hultberg, why not give David Johnson Elliott a "lay" or lease, since he had been an Alaskan missionary since 1891 and possessed no claims.[26]

Besides the friction between Anderson and Hultberg, another background factor should be mentioned. This was the increased hostility between Eric O. Lindblom and Hultberg. Lindblom had gotten the gold fever in San Francisco, signed up on a whaler for two years, jumped ship at Port Clarence, and had made his way with difficulty along the coast for one hundred and forty miles to Golovnin Bay. Grub-staked by Hultberg, he had gone to Council City and after working about

---

[25] Supreme Court of Illinois, October Term, 1904; *White Star Mining Company of Illinois* vs. *Nels O. Hultberg, The Swedish Evangelical Mission Covenant of America, Claes W. Johnson, Peter H. Anderson, Merchants' Loan and Trust Company, Abstract of Record*, pp. 5, 326, 331. Henceforth referred to as *Abstract of Record*.

[26] David Johnson changed his name to "Elliott" because of the great number of Johnsons. He served as a teacher with A. E. Karlson at Unalakleet until 1897.

one month had been persuaded by Hultberg to go to Nome. When Brynteson, Lindeberg, and Lindblom made their phenomenal discoveries, Lindblom became the owner of the largest number of claims. Because of the food, transportation and shelter given Lindblom, and because of an agreement made, Hultberg had some basis for believing that Lindblom had defrauded him. The result was a lawsuit instituted in San Francisco. Hultberg's friends turned against him, and the secretary of the Covenant telegraphed him about December 5, and wrote him a letter on December 9, seeking to dissuade him.[27]

One other background factor needs to be stressed. This was the anticipation by Covenant officials of substantially benefitting from the discovery of gold in Alaska. During the summer and fall of 1898 they had received letters from missionaries about the "rich gold discoveries made and expected to be found or made at Golovnin Bay." In the spring of 1899, Hultberg was in Chicago and he received there Anderson's letter of January 1 announcing the new strike at Nome. Before leaving Chicago Hultberg expressed "the certain expectation that before the year's end the Covenant's debt would be paid," and in a written report read to the annual conference at Des Moines, June, 1899, he spoke of the new discoveries of gold and other minerals.[28] This appetite for riches to be obtained was whetted still further by letters in the fall, evidently from Karlson and Hultberg, that Anderson was coming to Chicago with $50,000 from the Mission Claim.

The Beginning of the Controversy

Such was the situation in December, 1899, when Anderson arrived in Chicago. He first met with some of the school officials shortly before Christmas, at North Park College. The school officials were eager to know Anderson's plans for sharing some of the reported $50,000, but they did not question his ownership of No. 9 Above. Anderson gave no specific answer,

27 Lindblom had promised to give $15,000 to the Covenant. It was feared by some of the officials that if the lawsuit was continued, Lindblom would refuse to carry out his pledge.

28 *Förbundets Femtonde Årsmötes Rapport Till Församlingarna, Des Moines, Iowa, 1899,* p. 37. Hultberg did not read the report himself, since he had already left for Alaska.

but promised to do something, and shortly thereafter gave $10,000 to the Covenant.[29]

Under ordinary circumstances, Anderson's gift would have been highly appreciated. But to a committee expecting $50,000 Anderson's donation represented only one-fifth of the anticipated amount. Consequently, it was referred to as "a trifle." Anderson himself heard derogatory reports about his donation, and he received a letter informing him that there was a misunderstanding between him and the Covenant officials, that Brynteson and Karlson implied that he should have given more, and that he should come to Chicago in January to clear up the matter of No. 9 Above. Anderson sent a telegram to Chicago about January 5, 1900, and on the next day sent the following letter:

Enterprise, Kansas,
January 6, 1900.

Prof. D. Nyvall,
Chicago, Illinois.

DEAR BROTHER IN THE LORD: — Just arrived home from Salina, and sent a telegram to you. My wife and myself will come next Thursday. It surprises me very much that there is such a misunderstanding. You have heard the truth from me, and, before God, I know that I have acted right. And so far as No. 9 is concerned, I have nothing further to clear up. I only hope that both Carlson [A. E. Karlson] and Brynteson will remain, so that I can meet them together with the committee.

It pains me greatly that *my friends* not only mistrust me, but put me down entirely. Yet I am pleased that I have a good and clear conscience.

Fraternally,

P. H. Anderson.[30]

On January 19-20, 1900, the Covenant executive committee held its semi-annual meeting. Those present were C. A. Bjork, president, S. W. Sundberg, vice-president, David Nyvall, secretary, Axel Mellander, vice-secretary, and four trustees: S. A. Matson, C. G. Petterson, Charles Wallblom, and C. A. Young-

[29] *Abstract of Record,* pp. 268, 271.
[30] *Ibid.,* p. 428.

17

quist. Besides these, two Alaska missionaries were present, Anderson and Karlson. This was the first meeting at which the question of ownership of No. 9 Above was discussed. Anderson presented the story of the staking for the Eskimo boys, and the doubts about the right of Eskimos to hold claims, the second staking whereby Price staked No. 8 and No. 9 Above and sold the latter claim to Anderson for $20. Upon being asked why No. 9 Above was called the Mission Claim, Anderson replied that it was called the Religious Claim or Mission Claim because it was not worked on Sundays. Karlson expressed "his opinion" that the claim belonged to the Mission and asserted that the general opinion in Alaska was the same.[31]

A special meeting was held on February 7. The reason for this special meeting was that oral statements had been made by Brynteson which implied that the Covenant owned the mine. Youngquist had talked with Brynteson and told him that Anderson had turned over $10,000 to the Covenant. "Is that all?" said Brynteson. "Yes, that is all," replied Youngquist. Then Brynteson said, "Well, Mr. Anderson . . . has to turn over a number of tens of thousands to you people or to your Mission." Youngquist testified further that when he solicited funds from Brynteson for the cause of the Covenant, Brynteson parried, "Well, you must go for Mr. Anderson. He has got some more —he has got some gold there that belongs to the Mission, and when he has done right and turned over to you that what doesn't belong to him, why, then I will see what I can do and will do for the Mission." [32]

C. G. Petterson also testified of a conversation with Brynteson. "On February 6, 1900, I saw John Brynteson at Hartfelt's [Högfeldt?] in Chicago. I went up there at night because Anderson was out in North Park, and he wanted to speak to Brynteson. I told him, 'Anderson wants to see you.' They were running after him for money. Then I told him that Anderson had given $10,000 to the Mission. 'No. Well,' he says, 'Why? Why is that? $10,000? Why is that for? Well,' he said, 'he donated that. Oh.' he said, 'that is nothing. The claim No. 9,' he said, 'is belong to the Mission, and he took out there

31 *Ibid.*, pp. 303, 425 f.
32 *Ibid.*, p. 263.

—I saw the money in San Francisco—it was about $75,000 or $80,000.' And he said, 'He got to give anyway $20,000 more, and he could keep the other money,' he says, 'to work the claim next year.' 'Well,' I say, 'is that the case? Will you face that up.' I said, 'with Anderson? Will you go out with me to North Park tomorrow? When you go out there I will go with you, and I will take you out there if you don't know exactly the street car you shall take.' 'Yes, I will wait until you come tomorrow.' And I went there just about one o'clock on the day after, and took Brynteson along, and we went out to North Park." [33]

From these conversations, therefore, it is evident that Youngquist and Petterson were instrumental in the convening of a special meeting of the sub-committee which was held on February 7. Those present were Nyvall, Mellander, Youngquist, Petterson, Anderson and Brynteson.

If Youngquist and Petterson were hopeful that the meeting would provide a solution to the problem, they were disappointed. For Anderson was in no way overawed by the presence of Brynteson. Anderson claimed in the open meeting that No. 9 belonged to him personally. When the committee members turned to Brynteson, he confirmed the claim of Anderson by saying, "It is just as Anderson said." Pressed by Nyvall to state explicitly his views on the ownership, Brynteson repeated the story of the staking for the Eskimo boys, the restaking by Price, and the giving of No. 8 Above to Price as pay for the restaking of both No. 8 and No. 9 Above. At this point, Anderson objected to the idea that there was an agreement whereby Price would get No. 8 as a reward for restaking No. 9 and selling it to Anderson. If any such agreement had been made, it was not made between Anderson and Price, but between Price and the other members of the party.

Anderson had expressed surprise at the way his gift of $10,000 had been received. He had heard it referred to as a trifle. He probably was sensitive on this subject, therefore, when Brynteson suggested that Anderson should make a larger contribution to the Covenant. Anderson replied that he could

---

[33] *Ibid.*, pp. 252 f. The reader should keep in mind that Petterson's native language was Swedish, not English.

not give any more money at present because he had some law-suits in Alaska to worry about.[34] When Brynteson suggested that the Covenant might support Anderson in these lawsuits, Mellander said that such an arrangement would depend on the basic question of whether Anderson or the Covenant was to be considered the owner of No. 9 Above. Thus matters stood, and for the next few months there was no further agitation about the matter.

The Mining Season of 1900

The greatest stampede in Alaskan history occurred in the summer of 1900. In May before the ice had gone out of the Bering Sea, Nome had a population of approximately 4,000. By June 10, navigation was possible, and during the next seven weeks some 18,000 people were unceremoniously landed on the bleak shores of Nome.[35] These hapless and often helpless individuals were attracted to Nome by wild rumors of fortunes made. During the fall and winter of 1899-1900 they had read of the discovery of gold in the very beaches of Nome, of miners picking up nuggets on the strand as if they were boys gathering pebbles on the shore. Their appetites whetted still further by rosy golden pictures painted by transportation companies, these ordinary citizens spent their savings to reach Nome, only to find the beach worked out, the tundra and creeks staked for thirty miles, and the nuggets nowhere to be found.

Among those who arrived in this hectic period was Anderson, who had brought friends and relatives to Alaska to aid in working his mines. With increased transportation facilities, adequate supplies, sluice boxes, and a large labor force, prospects seemed to be bright for a successful season. Two conditions, however, need to be mentioned because of their adverse effect. One was the lack of water for the mines, especially in

34 O. José Comptois, a French doctor, had jumped No. 2 Above, and Paddy Ryan had jumped No. 9 Above. A temporary settlement had been effected when Judge Charles S. Johnson of Sitka came to Nome in August, 1899 (See Court Journal, No. 8, in the office of the clerk of the court, Juneau, Alaska, Case No. 1006).

35 Most estimates on the number of persons stampeding to Nome are exaggerated. The best estimate (18,000) is given by Lieutenant D. H. Jarvis, who served as port warden in 1900 (Nome Daily News, September 12, 1900, p. 1).

The man on the extreme right is S. G. Cronstedt, a brother-in-law of David Nyvall. Next to Cronstedt is Dr. A. G. Anderson, a brother of P. H. Anderson. Next to Dr. Anderson is John Forsling. The last man, unfortunately, remains unidentified.

Twenty-nine of the miners who worked on No. 9 Above in the most productive year—1900. The man with the pan of gold is Dr. A. G. Anderson. To the left is S. G. Cronstedt, and to the right is John Forsling, holding a revolver. The second man to the right of Forsling is Julius Ostberg, a cousin of P. H. Anderson.

June and July when the usual rains did not come. The other condition was the notorious legal complication resulting from a deeply-laid plot on the part of a small group of politicians to seize the mines in Anvil Creek from the "lucky Swedes." [36]

Ever since 1884 Alaska had been governed by the Oregon code. The stampedes to the Klondike, the Yukon diggings, and the Seward Peninsula had more than doubled the white population in the Territory. As the clamor for law increased, Congress responded by enacting "An Act Making Further Provision for Civil Government for Alaska, and for Other Purposes." This bill, which became law on June 6, 1900, provided for three judgeships and for three judicial districts, the second of which included the St. Michael and Nome area. Strong pressure was exerted upon senators, representatives, the attorney general, and even President McKinley for these positions, and especially for the Nome judgeship—the most coveted political plum. The ablest candidate was James Wickersham of Tacoma, Washington, who expected the Nome judgeship by means of the good offices of Senator A. G. Foster, but the successful candidate was Arthur H. Noyes of Minneapolis.[37] Aided by Alexander McKenzie, Republican State Chairman of North Dakota, Senator Henry Hansbrough of the same state, and by a host of recommendations from officials, judges, and politicians from Minnesota and North Dakota, Mr. Noyes was appointed by President McKinley in June.[38] He sailed for Nome on July 8, in the company of Alexander McKenzie, and landed at Nome, Saturday, July 21. Two days later, before any legal notice had been given of the opening of the court, even before a court room or a clerk's office had been established, Judge Noyes at his hotel had signed papers appointing his friend McKenzie

[36] The writer is preparing some articles on the machinations of Judge Arthur H. Noyes and Receiver Alexander McKenzie. These two men are thinly disguised in Rex Beach's novel, *The Spoilers,* as Judge Stillman and Receiver McNamara.

[37] I have been privileged to go through the appointment files in the Department of Justice records in the National Archives, Washington, D. C. Also, I have examined the personal diaries of Judge Wickersham, in the possession of his widow and niece at Juneau, Alaska. To Mrs. Wickersham and Ruth Coffin, I acknowledge my deep gratitude.

[38] On June 8, 1900, Judge-elect Wickersham received the following telegram from Senator Foster: "Indications you will be assigned to Eagle City. Tremendous pressure assign Brown Juneau and Noyes Nome" (MS. Diary of James Wickersham, June 8, 1900).

receiver of six of the richest mines on Anvil Creek. On the evening of July 23 McKenzie drove with horse and wagon four miles out to Anvil Creek and took possession as receiver. When the real owners through their lawyers protested this high-handed act, their exceptions were disallowed by Judge Noyes, and when they asked for an appeal, they were told that there could be no appeal from an interlocutory order. Tension mounted, tempers became strained, and in every saloon and restaurant miners talked of "King McKenzie" and his pliant tool, Judge Noyes.[39]

Among the mines seized by McKenzie was No. 2 Above, belonging to Anderson. The original contestant was O. José Comptois, a French doctor from Council City, who had jumped No. 2 Above in December, 1898. Using the lame allegation that powers of attorney were illegal, Comptois had lost his case before Commissioner Shephard in March, 1899, and before Judge Charles S. Johnson in August, 1899. Despite these legal rebuffs, Comptois conveyed his "right" to McKenzie's law firm, Hubbard, Beeman, and Hume, for a consideration. It was this notorious legal firm, plus Judge Noyes, plus Receiver McKenzie, with whom Anderson's lawyers had to deal.[40]

Besides the trouble with Receiver McKenzie, Anderson had other difficulties during the summer of 1900. One of the trying problems he had to deal with was the mismanagement and inefficiency of David Johnson Elliott. Elliott had been a teacher at the station at Unalakleet from 1891 to 1897. Returning to Nome in 1899, he had been given a lease of 165 feet of ground on the lower part of No. 9 Above. During 1899 and 1900 he had carried on his mining operations, according to Anderson, in an unminerlike fashion. He further incurred the wrath of Anderson by his conduct during the winter of 1899-1900. Since Elliott remained in Nome all winter, he had been left in charge of the affairs of the Pioneer Mining Company. Because of the great sickness at Nome, Elliott had given money freely

[39] See *The Case of Judge Arthur H. Noyes,* a pamphlet in the National Archives, Department of Justice, File 10,000 (1900).

[40] Judge Ross of the United States Circuit Court of Appeals, Ninth Circuit said: "There is but one conclusion to be drawn from such proceedings, and that is that the appointment of a receiver to work and mine the placer claim owned by the defendant was the beginning and the end of the cause of action." See *Anderson v. Comptois,* 1 *Alaska Federal Reports.*

for a hospital building, paid doctors' bills for deserving and undeserving patients, supplied some of the camps with food without securing receipts, and outfitted prospectors, the cost of which he partly charged to Anderson's account. His naivete and lack of business acumen were expensive, since he had used up between $30,000-$40,000 of other people's money. It is understandable, therefore, why Anderson was "pretty hot about the matter and provoked." The matter was brought "before the U. S. Marshall or some other U. S. officer up there," and Elliott found it necessary to convey his portion of No. 9 Above to his creditors.[41]

Another difficulty must have caused Anderson considerable worry. Shortly before he left Alaska, he was served with a summons, to justify his possession of No. 9 Above. This summons came from William A. Gilmore, an attorney in Nome. Gilmore had been consulted by O. P. Anderson, who had recently arrived in northern Alaska as the new Covenant missionary. Armed with a power of attorney from the Covenant, and probably from the Good Hope Mining Company also, O. P. Anderson had initiated another legal inquiry which was to cause considerable difficulty and embarrassment to the Covenant in the years to come.[42]

Despite these difficulties, Anderson experienced a very successful mining season. It was fortunate that No. 9 was not jumped. It had been jumped in 1899 by Paddy Ryan, but his suit was unsuccessful. During the summer of 1900, therefore, No. 9 Above prospered. A corps of about thirty-five miners lived in tents on the premises, and worked in two twelve-hour shifts, night and day. Standard pay was $5 a day, plus board and "room" in a tent.[43] By the end of the season, No. 9 Above had produced $175,000 in net proceeds.[44]

[41] *Abstract of Record,* pp. 246, 248.

[42] In 1902 Attorney Gilmore sued the Covenant for $25,000. It is difficult to see any justification for this sum, but attorneys in Alaska demanded extortionate fees. See Covenant Sub-Committee Minutes, 1901-1904, for August 6, 1901, January 7, 1902, and March 4, 1902. These minutes are in the Covenant archives. Referred to hereafter as Sub-Committee Minutes.

[43] Data obtained from a letter of S. G. Cronstedt, who worked on No. 9 Above in 1900.

[44] MS. Record, p. 138. See also *Nels O. Hultberg and Swedish Evangelical Mission Covenant of America v. Peter H. Anderson et. al.* The Supreme Court of Illinois, June term, 1911, No. 7712, *Brief and Argument for Plain-*

So far as the Covenant was concerned, the issues on No. 9 Above were held in abeyance until the fall of 1900. When P. H. Anderson returned from his successful season in Alaska, however, it was natural that the Covenant officials desired some kind of statement from him. At a meeting held at Professor Nyvall's home, in December, 1900, Anderson was asked to make a report. He promised to send in an offer to the semi-annual meeting, scheduled to be held within two months.

In January, 1901, the officers of the Covenant decided to consult with Axel Chytraus, one of the judges of the Superior Court of Cook County. The occasion for this conference was a letter which the Covenant had received from William A. Gilmore, the attorney in Nome, Alaska, who had been consulted by O. P. Anderson. After consulting with the Covenant officials, Judge Chytraus wrote the following letter to Professor Nyvall:

Law Office of Deneen & Hamill,
160 Washington St.

Chicago,
January 12, 1901.

My Dear Prof.:

Owing to the pressure of other matters, I laid aside the documents you left with me in regard to the claim of the Swedish Evangelical Mission Covenant of America *vs.* Rev. P. H. Anderson, who was a missionary in the employ of the Swedish Mission at Golovin Bay in 1898.

I have carefully read the communication of William A. Gilmore in regard to claim No. 9, on Anvil Creek. The matter is very important, and requires serious consideration. However, I have arrived at the conclusion that, if the facts can be proven as stated in Mr. Gilmore's communication, in regard to the locating of the claim by the two young native men for the Mission, and that with the consent of the native boys, and upon representations to them shown in the communication, the claims were located in the names of G. W. & R. L. Price, I have no doubt but what the claim No. 9 can be recovered for the Covenant.

tiffs in Error, p. 119. On one occasion Anderson testified that $175,000 was a mistaken estimate, and that $125,000 would be more accurate.

It seems from the communication from Mr. Gilmore that G. W. Price, for himself and his brother, for whom he acted in locating the claim, stated that he would deed the claim to Rev. P. H. Anderson "in trust for the Mission." When this is established by evidence, then the Rev. P. H. Anderson's personal interest in the claim ceases. It is stated that, as further evidence of this fact, in addition to the testimony of those present, it can be shown that the Rev. P. H. Anderson has told many people that he has held the claim in trust for the Mission.

Although the matter is a serious one, it seems to me that you are not only justified but required, as a matter of duty, to institute proceedings for the recovery of what belongs to the Covenant. Some inquiry should, perhaps, be made in regard to what G. W. Price would say, as he would be a very important, if not the most important, witness.

Very truly yours,
Axel Chytraus.[45]

This letter of Judge Chytraus, with its suggestion that the Covenant was not only justified but required to institute proceedings for the recovery of No. 9 Above, was based on the supposition that Anderson held it "in trust for the Mission." Since this had been the real point at issue for more than a year, the letter did not clarify the issue, but it did supply a motive for legal sanctions.

Anderson had promised in December to send in a report of what he would give to the Covenant. This promise was fulfilled when he sent the following two letters:

Oakland, Cal.,
Feb. 7, 1901.

To the Com. of the Covenant:

Beloved Bros. in the Lord, God's Peace.

I will hereby announce that I donate $25,000 to the Covenant's school, and $4,000 to the fund for students of theology. Also $25,000 to a hospital in Lake View or some other growing place within the city. It is now my wish that these means be used for the above mentioned pur-

---

[45] MS. Record, pp. 1430 f.

poses. But should the Covenant not desire a new hospital, then we will, in the future, determine for what Mission branches, within the Covenant, they can be of the greatest service. My desire is to awaken among our people an interest for a hospital. May God bless you in all, that his will may be done, and then will the work of the Covenant progress.

Brotherly,

P. H. Anderson.

P. S.—I have heard reports to the effect that the committee proposes to bring suit against me in regard to claim No. 9. If that is so, then I withdraw the above mentioned donations, and before I turn them over I desire a writing from you that such is not the fact.[46]

Oakland, Cal.,
Feb. 8, 1901.

Prof. D. Nyvall,
Chicago, Illinois.

My dear Brother in the Lord. God's Peace.

I sent you a letter for the Committee yesterday and the conditions for the donations. Now the conditions are that there shall be no more trouble from the Covenant Officials' side. I forgot to mention that I was served with a summons on account of No. 9 before I left Alaska last fall, so that if you commence troubling, you will not only have me, but also the trouble-makers in Alaska to litigate with. I fear nothing from your side other than the unpleasantness that follows a law suit, and also the expenses for attorneys.

I have seen in the papers that Aug. Anderson desires to again go to Alaska as a missionary. Now I will not make any suggestion to you, but I will, nevertheless, express my thoughts in regard to him as a missionary. The knowledge I obtained concerning him, while we were in Alaska, made such impression on me that I cannot refrain from expressing my thought that I do not consider him fit. Many have said to me that he is not right in his mind. This I will not say concerning him, but he is certainly

[46] *Abstract of Record,* p. 279.

rather queer, and he does not understand the language sufficient to teach. If such men are sent into the mission field, I cannot take any interest in that branch of the mission work.

May God bless you in the selection of missionaries for the heathen field.

My wife joins with me in the most sincere regards to you and your family.

Fraternally,

P. H. Anderson.[47]

When the members of the executive committee met at the Covenant church in Humboldt Park, February 13-16, 1901, they were confronted with difficult problems. They had just received Anderson's offer, and they were in possession of Gilmore's and Chytraus' communications. After discussing Anderson's offer of $54,000, they decided to reject this proposition. Instead, they countered with a demand for $100,000 and one-half of all future net proceeds from No. 9 Above. The executive committee decided that if Anderson's reply was favorable the sub-committee should recommend this settlement to the annual meeting. If Anderson's reply was unfavorable, the matter should be referred to a special meeting of the full executive committee.

On February 23, just a week after the adjournment of the executive committee, Nyvall wrote to Anderson, informing him of the decisions made. Although this letter is not available, we can guess its contents from the decisions made by the committee and from the following reply:

Oakland, Cal.,
March 12, 1901.

Prof. D. Nyvall,
Chicago, Ill.

My dear brother in Christ:

Your letter of the 23d ult. at hand. I know that it is a part of experience of mankind to hear rumors from time to time. It is not, however, pleasant to hear unpleasant reports about one's self. Still more unpleasant is the

[47] *Ibid.*, pp. 429 f.

rumor or statement where you are not advised as to the source or foundation. When the state or condition arises that has arisen here and between us it is much better to meet the apparent disagreement at the threshold and settle it than allow things to run along from time to time. Short settlements make long friends and *vice versa.* I have, therefore, concluded that it would be unwise in me and most unjust to myself to allow any claim to exist against me on the part of any one. I have a strong desire to help in the field of Christianity, and wish to do the same through you, but I do not see how I can do so if you have the right to command or require me to do anything financially. If money were given to you by me, as the matter stands now, it would be claimed that it was your money and not my gift. It would be immaterial, except for the reflection on myself, who owned the money so long as it did good; but I must decline to do anything until you have run these rumors to earth and have thoroughly exonerated me. When that is done I can give; until that is done I have something which belongs to you, but which I will not give you. In short, my position is that I owe you nothing, and that you have no claims upon me whatsoever.

Very sincerely,

P. H. Anderson.[48]

Anderson's reply was received about March 16-17. The sub-committee discussed this letter on March 19, but arrived at no conclusion. The real issue was whether Anderson's offers should be regarded as gifts, as he believed, or as settlements, as the committee believed. Since Anderson's reply was unfavorable, the sub-committee called a special meeting, in accordance with the decision of the executive committee, to be held on April 1 at the Mission Church on the north side of Chicago.

When the executive committee met on April 1, six members were present. Anderson's letter was read. His insistence on being cleared of unpleasant rumors and on his making a voluntary donation rather than a settlement were discussed. Then, upon the motion of C. G. Petterson, the committee

48 *Ibid.,* 431 f.

unanimously voted to revoke the decision of the semi-annual meeting asking for $100,000 plus a future 50% contingency sum. Instead, the committee decided to "hereafter consider P. H. Anderson's proposition as a voluntary donation, and consequently regard the matter against him settled, with mutual confidence and mutual friendship." To this proposition trustee S. A. Matson gave a later oral consent, but the two absent trustees from Minneapolis, Charles Wallbom and Aaron Carlson, wrote letters urging the committee to stand by its previous February decision and also to refer the matter to the forthcoming annual meeting. They did not, however, care to reserve themselves further against the April 1 decision of the committee.[49]

The committee decided further to publicize the propositions of Anderson and also that of John Brynteson. Of Anderson's donation, $29,000 was designated for North Park College, and $25,000 for a hospital. Brynteson's proposition was to donate another $25,000 for the hospital with the understanding that it be built in Lake View, Chicago. The committee publicized its acceptance on behalf of the Covenant of the $29,000 for the school, but it referred the donations for a hospital to the annual meeting.

It must have been with a real sigh of relief that the secretary, Nyvall, wrote to Anderson of the new decisions made by the committee. Two days after the meeting, he penned the following letter:

Chicago, Ill.,
April 3, 1901.

Brother P. H. Anderson,
Oakland, Cal.

My dear Brother: God's Peace!

First and foremost, I desire, on behalf of myself and the Committee, to most heartily thank you for your brotherly kindness towards our friends Andres, at their arrival in San Francisco. God will reward you for the interest you show in His concerns and His service.

Furthermore, I have today an unexpected and for me personally a very pleasant commission, viz.: To inform

[49] *Ibid.*, p. 433.

29

you, that the Executive Committee, by reason of the information and, as we believe, a better understanding of matters and things, has arrived at the conclusion in all respects to take you at your word and entirely dismiss all suspicion and all wondering with reference to the points of misunderstanding existing between us. We now see the matter thus. That you, the same as our other brothers from Alaska, make voluntary donations to the Covenant's work, and that no cause exists on our side to demand settlement. We, as the Covenant's Executive Committee, lay down every claim in that regard, and declare ourselves willing to receive your donations as they are given, with the confidence and the brotherly understanding that you, as you say, have a strong desire with your means, which the Lord has given you, to advance his cause and to do so through the Covenant. It will undoubtedly surprise you, that we now so suddenly arrive at this conclusion, and I myself feel almost a little surprise to be permitted as Secretary, to report such a turn of things; but you must remember that at the bottom it has, during the whole time, been our greatest desire to be able to see the matter from that point of view, and that we have not considered ourselves able to do so, you will certainly not be surprised at if you only know the sources whence information and claims and accusations and demands have come to the Committee, directed against you. In that regard I will only say that they have come from many directions and near points. But enough in that matter. We have, by the Committee's resolution, arrived at the conclusion that we ought to give up claims and in place thereof depend upon such interest as we have found in you, and we believe that in that manner we serve our work best; and we are ready to go to the Covenant with a report in which we thankfully acknowledge the receipt of your proposition to the school and the hospital exactly as you have presented them to the semi-annual meeting. I needn't say, that to me personally, this is a very gratifying solution of this matter, which, during a period of over a year, has been a never ceasing nightmare for me and my colleagues on the Committee.

And I cannot thank God sincerely enough that we now have arrived at the conclusions to act in personal confidence and friendship in this matter, at the same time, it is my sincere and confident hope that you will nobly and as a Christian mission friend use this victory that you now have, if I may so express myself, and that being left entirely free to regard your gifts to the Covenant as voluntary donations you will do exactly as your heart most nobly and best, urges you to. And, in that connection, I desire especially to thank you for that point in your proposition to the semi-annual meeting, wherein, in regard to the donation to the hospital work, you add the sentence: That if the Covenant shall not determine to build a hospital, it may then be determined for what purpose, the donations shall be used. I assure you that this liberal-mindedness and disinterestedness shall in the highest recommend you before our Mission's true friends, and gladden their hearts. I have written lengthily to Bro. Brynteson with reference to the apprehensions of the Covenant's Committee, regarding the great undertaking which our esteemed friend Dr. Johnson so strives for, and I requested him to inform you of the contents of that letter. I can assure you that we shall please you and Brynteson in all respects in which it is possible, consonant with our ripened judgment in regard to what will best benefit that mission work which we have received in charge to advance. In that regard, I have written, as stated, fully to Bro. Brynteson. We shall now proceed to present before the Christian public as widely and broadly as we can, what you, Brethren, so munificently and kindly have offered to do for the Mission, and we shall gladly and without any reservation give you all that credit which you so richly and well deserve for this generosity, and we hope that hereafter no misunderstanding shall arise between us, but that on the contrary, we shall have occasion in complete harmony and undisturbed happiness to co-operate for the best of the missions of the Covenant. I speak in this matter with a heart filled to overflowing, and nothing would please me more, than if through this brotherly understanding our beloved missions would receive a lift whereby we should overcome not only present difficulties, but in the continuance would be enabled to prepare ourselves for a more vigorous and extensive work.

What we might do in that respect in Canada, Montana, Texas, I have written more than once, and I mention it even now in this connection. My fixed opinion is that if we follow the calls of the Lord in the cries of distress from the fields of darkness, we shall, within five years, see a strengthening of our Mission forces such as we now can hardly dream of or hope for. In the work itself, we need a revival here at home, to follow out, with vigor and progress the important outside Mission charges which the Lord has given us. Thus, I have performed my commission and send to you the executive committee's hearty and brotherly greeting, and I hope, that you, who so patiently has submitted to criticisms and discussions in this delicate matter will, with entire and brotherly confidence, accept this extended hand.

Yours in the Lord,
Heartily affectionate,

D. Nyvall.

P. S.—It is now decided that our half-yearly meeting shall be held in Duluth, Minnesota, during mid-summer. I earnestly hope that you can so arrange as to be with us then.[50]

On April 6, Anderson wrote a letter wherein he requested that his initial offer be accepted or rejected unconditionally. His offer had been held up for two months, and he was uncertain of the sources of the accusations against him. The following letter, with its insistence on immediate action, must be read against that background. Nyvall's letter of April 3 probably did not reach him until April 8 at the earliest.

Oakland, Cal.,
April 6, 1901.

Prof. D. Nyvall,
Chicago, Ill.

My Dear Brother in Christ:

Acknowledging receipt of your favor of the 23rd ult. I would say that I cannot at present say as to my ability to go to the meeting to be held in Duluth the latter part

---

[50] MS. Record, pp. 1827-1832.

of June. I would like to go to the meeting, but it is so far off that I cannot tell just now. I want to avoid going to Alaska if I can do so until July, but I think our matters should be disposed of at once. I don't know why a postponement should be had and the committee certainly has the power and can exercise the right if it chooses. Human life is very uncertain at the best and I must insist that you act in this matter at once. It is certain that the offer I made you is a good one or a bad one and I desire it to be accepted or rejected absolutely and unconditionally and at once. You have had ample time to verify the rumors that reached you respecting myself, while I am not even made aware of the names of the authors of these stories. I am given no chance to protect myself and my assailants are protected, apparently, by those whom I desire to benefit. Looking from my standpoint this is hardly Christianlike and the injustice of the situation worries me. I must be accepted as a friend or an enemy and my accusers must be supported or repudiated by you. Believing that my conduct in the past should merit a speedy judgment upon your part that I have been imposed upon by some one, but that I again have your full confidence, I remain

Yours,

P. H. Anderson.[51]

After writing this letter, Anderson received Nyvall's letter of April 3. Naturally, Anderson was pleased with the decision of the executive committee, and he expressed his satisfaction in the following letter:

Oakland, Calif.,
April 22nd, 1901.

Prof. D. Nyvall,
Chicago, Ill.

My dear Brother in Christ:

I beg to acknowledge receipt of your favor of April 3rd and its contents pleases me. I am very glad to know you have come to the same conclusion which I had considered the true and just one all along. Inasmuch as there has been misunderstanding of the situation heretofore

---

[51] *Abstract of Record*, p. 438.

would you not kindly send me a release from any and all claims against myself or any properties that I may own. This will avoid any possibility of such a controversy ever coming up again and possibly cause useless ill-feeling and expense to both of us. Upon such a document I shall be only too glad to make such donations to the Covenant and its work as I had heretofore intended to, but I must have a general release from any claim or pretended claim before doing so. I trust you will appreciate that this is purely a business proposition on my part to protect myself and family in the future, and that there is no personal feeling whatever in the matter; on the contrary my heart is as much in the work of the Society as it has always been.

Another matter which I think is unjust and can easily be remedied occurs to me. In an issue of the Mission Friend the Editor has taken occasion to criticise the conduct of all Alaska Missionaries or friends as he calls them. I am one of those of whom he writes and I believe it would be but fair to have him retract, by an article, the impression carried by his former article or statement. I hope you can have this done.

This is to the Committee, but I send it to you.

Very Truly Yours,

P. H. Anderson.[52]

The significant point about this letter is not the resentment against the criticism expressed in *Missions-Vännen*, but the request for a general release from any claim or pretended claim. Nyvall's letter of April 3 constituted an informal release, but Anderson insisted on a formal release which would be legally binding.

When Nyvall received Anderson's letter, he must have felt that his hope for a prompt settlement was premature. He had said frankly that this problem had been "a never ceasing nightmare for me and my colleagues on the committee." Once more, the problem seemed to be reopened, and the nightmare returned. With a heavy heart he wrote back a reply:

[52] MS. Record, pp. 1834 f.

[Chicago, Illinois]
May 9, 1901

[To P. H. Anderson]

Your last letter made me real sad, and I will tell you why. In my opinion we could not as a committee do you greater harm before public opinion than to give you such a release as you demand in your letter. It is of course self-evident that if the Covenant's committee prepares such a document there would be in that a confession by us that we consider the Covenant has rights which we in the meantime on behalf of the Covenant surrender. Hence I wish that you sincerely consider this matter, and that it is absolutely impossible for the Covenant committee to go before the annual conference with a report of that purport that we have given to you or anybody else a release of claim, as that would imply that we say at the same time that we have demands, and at the same time acknowledge that we don't make these demands effective. If we come before the Covenant's annual conference with a report of that purport, it would not only be impossible for us to defend our position, but we would also have given you a very poor testimonial before the whole Christendom. This cannot and it ought not to happen.

[D. Nyvall][53]

The question of giving Anderson a release remained an open question when the executive committee met at Duluth on June 19, 1901. This committee approved of the minutes of the meetings held from February 13, both of the semi-annual meeting, the sub-committee meetings, and the special session of the semi-annual meeting, the sub-committee meetings, and the special session of the executive committee. It then proceeded to establish the order of business for the annual conference scheduled to begin the following day. The eleventh item of business provided "that the Covenant ratify the decision of the executive committee that on behalf of the Covenant they receive a donation of $25,000 to the school and $4,000 as a fund for the indigent students of the theology." The twelfth item specified that of the $25,000 a sum not exceeding $20,000 be ex-

---

[53] *Abstract of Record*, p. 455.

pended for school buildings, such as a dormitory, a president's home, and possibly an auditorium.

On June 21, after an entire session devoted to the question of building a hospital, the annual meeting voted to accept with thanks the offer of Brynteson and Anderson of $25,000 each. On June 22 the delegates approved of the recommendation of the executive committee to accept Anderson's donation of $29,000 for the school, and expressed their thanks by standing up.[54] This decision was made after a frank discussion of the question of No. 9 Above. Aaron Carlson particularly expressed his conviction that No. 9 Above belonged to the Covenant, and Mellander argued that both Brynteson and Anderson were under obligation to the Covenant. Therefore, he contended, there was no need to let these donors control the delegates. In the discussion "the language was pretty strong." "Explosions occurred, and occasionally it was rather hot." In private conversation at the conference, Dr. Johnson called the trustees fools because they did not proceed with the building of the hospital.

The annual meeting adjourned on June 24. Two days later Nyvall reported the decisions of the conference in the following letter:

Chicago, Ill.,
26 June, 1901.

My Dear Brother P. H. Anderson,
Oakland, Cal.:

God's Peace.

I have the great pleasure to report that the annual meeting in Duluth thankfully received yours and Brynteson's donations to be used according to your wish. Regarding the hospital, a committee was appointed, with the friend of the hospital, C. Flodin, as president, with full power to receive donations in continuance and proceed as fast as the plan has so far matured that it can be done without going into debt. I hope that this is now entirely satisfactory and may the Lord direct it all in His Honor and to the happiness of all of us.

[54] *Förbundets 17:de Årsmötes i Duluth, Minnesota, Rapport till Församlingarna, 1900*, pp. 109, 113.

No. 9 Above on Anvil Creek. S. G. Cronstedt is the man second to the left of the young man standing on the pile. Note the eight tents, including the large tent used as an eating place. Note also the tailings, hose, shovels, boots, and clothes.

Nome in 1899.

With reference particularly to your donations, I have the unmitigated pleasure to report that the resolution of the annual meeting constitutes in all respects a vote of confidence. First and foremost, the annual meeting have adopted, without opposition of any kind, the motion of the executive committee that your proposition be received *as a voluntary donation,* and the meeting expressed its thankfulness by voting in favor thereof by a rising vote. Further, the meeting authorized the executive committee to use the donation (or more correctly $20,000 thereof), for necessary buildings and repairs, viz.: First and foremost a dormitory and a home for the superintendent. These buildings would be rent-bringing. Further, if possible, also an auditorium. I hope now that you feel satisfied and content with this arrangement. Let us hear from you at the earliest. It must also be mentioned that it was resolved to receive the land company's proposition regarding a clear title to the property immediately, and the annual meeting assumed the indebtedness for which at the annual meeting there was subscribed something over $4,000. It is hoped that the whole can be obtained as we now have prospects of having everything satisfactorily arranged. In that respect, this annual meeting was of such great importance that it can never be overestimated. That which, during years, had been lying heavy and oppressed on the minds, had then free and open expression. Many explosions occurred and occasionally it was rather hot. But remarkable to say, it ended with such unanimous resolutions that I cannot remember any annual meeting at which we, in regard to such important and difficult matter, have acted so unanimously.

I cannot express how thankful to the Lord I am for the outcome in these matters. *I now perceive a clear road before us.* Internal confidence can again obtain, and the work be taken up with vigor and happiness. I would desire to write much more, but it is a little uncomfortable in traveling as I am, to do so.

We have organized a Mission Band within the school to, if possible, support a missionary in China to assist Matson. We have secured yearly subscriptions of about $200, but need $400. In addition we need a present sum of $200 for outfit and traveling expenses. Only teachers, students and alumni of our school are eligible for membership. Can we count on you?

Pardon me that I also come with a personal matter. I have during many years wished to be able to publish a greater collection of speeches. Talks to the Young and Missionary Folks, and some other things in the interest to the school, part in Swedish and part in English. But I lack the means. Have you not the inclination to make a loan to me for that purpose, in some way or another? It might be done through the Covenant's Book Concern if you, for example, were inclined to put in there a small sum, especially for that purpose. Perhaps thereby even that branch would be promoted. This matter I only mention. If you are inclined in that direction, I believe that with little risk a Covenant's Book Business might be built up. The little book business we have heretofore conducted has been paying. Had we only some resources to begin with, it would be comparatively easy to turn our people to our store for books. Our publication would thereby receive a greater circulation and in consequence of the greater circulation aid the book store. This, however, is only a suggestion.

Let us now, in Jesus' name, forget that which is past and reach for that which is before us, and pursue our purpose according to the call received from above in Christ Jesus. I am pleased, more pleased than I can express, too, now, on behalf of the whole work, be permitted, figuratively speaking, to embrace you in most brotherly understanding. I beg to be remembered to your wife. I believe that she will not be the least happy over this sunshine, which the Lord has sent us after the storm. A sincere greeting from my wife, who is with me on the journey to Minneapolis and to-day follows to Red Wing.

Yours sincerely,

D. Nyvall.[55]

Anderson replied to this letter about two weeks later, as follows:

[55] MS. Record, pp. 1841-1843.

Oakland, California,
July 13, 1901.

My Dear Brother, D. Nyvall,

God's Peace.

Thanks for the letter of the 26th of June. Glad to see
that it went so well at the meeting and that peace and love
was permitted to reign. The Lord be praised for all. I
have many times wished to be along at the Covenant's
annual meetings, and this year I thought there would be
an opportunity, as I would not go to Alaska. But even
this year I was hindered. My dear wife became ill so that
I was obliged to remain at home. She underwent an operation in the beginning of June and we believed succeeded
admirably, and she got up and went about a little. Hence
on June 25th, I went to Kansas for a short visit and when
last Tuesday I returned, to my surprise, I found that my
wife was ill again, so last Tuesday she was obliged to
again undergo an operation. She is now quite well and we
have the best of hope that she will entirely recover. It
has been a very trying period for me, but, thanks to God,
that it has gone as well as it has.

It has pleased me to see that everything went so well
at the meeting. I was a little doubtful in regard to the
hospital matter. I hope that it may go well and that we
may receive many large donations and that it may win a
general interest among our friends.

Yes, I am fully satisfied with what was determined
upon in regard to the school's money. It has always been
my wish that the Covenant should obtain a good school.

How is it with the $1,000.00 that I sent which should
be used for indigent theological students? I have not seen
nor heard that any thereof has been used for that purpose.
Was nothing said about the $4,000.00 or how the theo-
logical students should obtain the benefit thereof?

In regard to the release I require, before I send the
money you say that you regret this, my request. But I
cannot understand that you should regret it, because it is,
as we usually say in English, a "business proposition."
In consequence of the treatment I have received by the
Committee and the rumors I have heard, and the treatment Hagelin received and that from the leading men of

39

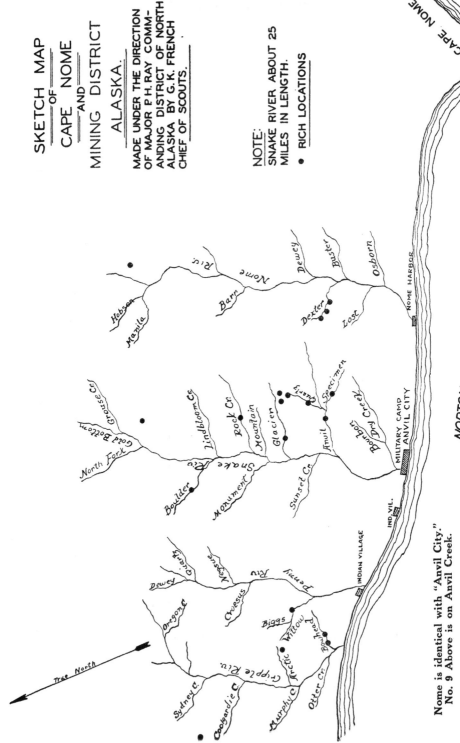

SKETCH MAP
OF
CAPE NOME
AND
MINING DISTRICT
ALASKA.

MADE UNDER THE DIRECTION OF MAJOR P.H. RAY COMMANDING DISTRICT OF NORTH ALASKA BY G.K. FRENCH CHIEF OF SCOUTS.

NOTE:
SNAKE RIVER ABOUT 25 MILES IN LENGTH.
• RICH LOCATIONS

True North

NORTON SOUND

CAPE NOME

Nome is identical with "Anvil City."
No. 9 Above is on Anvil Creek.

the Executive Committee, has occasioned that I demand a release. Hagelin's trouble I consider as the greatest scandal of the Good Hope Mining Company. In my opinion, they are worse than McKenzie. You seem to think that I fear that, under favorable circumstances, the Covenant would open up the controversy again. I have absolutely no fear that the Covenant might obtain a more favorable opportunity to present its case. McKenzie had not the slightest right with our matters in Alaska, but nevertheless he occasioned us not so little trouble and expense. So, although without any rights, one can occasion law suits. I enclose herewith a release that I wish signed by the officers. I hope that you, as the officers, perceive the importance of this for me, after I have heard as much as I have heard.

I have just read in the *Minneapolis Veckoblad* that, at the meeting, it was discussed whether my donation to the School was given on condition that the school's debt should be paid this year. My dear Brother, wherefrom has this come? You have my letter and conditions and if that question was presented it was a deception of the North Park crowd in order to gain its points. Let the *Minneapolis Veckoblad* learn the truth.

It is too bad that it is so far to Chicago. I should be pleased to make a trip there. We will see if I cannot make a visit there this fall.

Perhaps I should mention that our minister has resigned and accepted a call to San Francisco and we will now have to look for another. Have you any one that you can recommend?

May the Lord's blessing rest on us all.

Fraternally,

P. H. Anderson.[56]

Evidently this letter was slow in arriving, because Nyvall telegraphed on July 24 that he had received no reply to his letter of June 26. Anderson sent another letter, consequently, the following day:

[56] *Abstract of Record,* pp. 446 f.

Oakland, California,
July 25, 1901.

Professor D. Nyvall,
Chicago, Illinois.

My beloved Brother in the Lord: God's Peace.

I was somewhat surprised yesterday evening when I received a telegram from you to the effect that you had not received my letter. I was beginning to expect a letter from you. I don't know why I made no copy of my letter. I will now, therefore, write a new one. I have nearly forgotten what I wrote in my former letter, but in your last letter I observed that you became displeased because I requested a release and seemed to believe that I fear that, at a favorable opportunity, the Covenant would take up the case against me. I do not fear any such opportunities; because I consider myself to stand upon righteous and lawful ground with my affairs, but without the Covenant having any rights against me, it might occasion trouble and expenses. McKenzie had no right against our claims up there, but he could nevertheless bring us into a terrible snarl and put us to extra expenses. So that, without having rights, one can start law suits. And, considering all I have heard and seen of some of our officials, not so much in regard to my own affairs, but more particularly regarding Hagelin's, that I regard as the greatest scandal of anything I am aware of in Alaska. Indeed, it is sad to think there are Christians, and particularly that our leaders have occasioned this. Had not such an attitude been assumed towards us then there, I would not have asked for a release, especially now that the committee has declared itself not to have any right or demand upon me. And you understand as well as I do that a release does not involve the least renunciation of any rights, and you as a committee have acknowledged that you were mistaken through rumors,—what then hinders my receiving it? I enclose a blank which I desire you and the President to sign. Then I will at the earliest send the money, in order that the work upon the new buildings may begin. It grieves me that such an estranged condition should have existed between us. But your last letters made both myself and

42

wife feel good and, therefore, I will forget the past, and, in Brotherly love, work together.

I would have wished that you, together with your father, had made a trip here. And I understand from your letter of last winter that you expected to take a trip to the West coast. You will be heartily welcome if you come. I will further ask if a recommendation from me will be sufficient for a Brother who desires to enter the Seminary? Pastor A. Anderson would give him one, but, of course, he desires that he should go to Professor Risberg's school.

Hope that this letter will occasion no feeling, because I desire the best relations to exist between us.

My wife has had two operations in a short time, so that we have had a very trying time. She is now able to be up occasionally and we now believe she will be fully restored.

With the heartiest regards of myself and wife,
Brotherly,

P. H. Anderson.[57]

The release which was enclosed was received by Nyvall, who signed it as secretary and sent it to President Bjork about July 30. Bjork consulted with Youngquist, the treasurer, and they decided to consult with Judge Chytraus about the matter. After reading the release, Chytraus said: "Well, you may as well sign it and send it, because it is of no value, and you may as well sign it and send it back where it came from." Bjork then signed the release and sent it to Anderson.[58]

When Anderson received the release on August 6, he objected to its form. Consequently, he wrote back the following letter:

Oakland, California,
August 6, 1901.

Pastor C. A. Bjork,
Chicago, Illinois.

Beloved Brother in the Lord. Peace.

Thanks for the letter that I have just received. It is true and correct that you shall understand that the money

[57] MS. Record, pp. 1895-1897.
[58] *Abstract of Record,* pp. 302 f.

43

that I propose to give shall be given as a donation, but as this release is written that will not be given as a donation, as the release is, it will cost $55,000.00. It would, of course, be all the same to me as long as I have it, but in event that no hospital should be built, I would have nothing to say regarding the $25,000.00 for the hospital. Therefore, I send another release in order to have the amount changed. In place of $55,000.00 will be written $1.00, and then it will be a donation that I give. Hoping that you will understand me correctly, and that it will not arouse any misunderstanding.

Brotherly,

P. H. Anderson.[59]

The second release was received from Anderson about August 11, and on August 16 was signed, sealed, and notarized, as follows:

KNOW ALL MEN BY THESE PRESENTS: KNOW YE,

That the Swedish Evangelical Covenant of America, a corporation organized and existing under and by virtue of the laws of the United States of America, whose principal place of business is in the City of Chicago, State of Illinois, for and in consideration of the sum of One Dollar lawful money of the United States of America, to it in hand paid by P. H. Anderson, of Alameda County, State of California, has remised, released, and forever discharged, and by these presents does for itself, its successors and assigns, remise, release and forever discharge the said P. H. Anderson, his heirs, executors and administrators, of and from all, and all manner of action and actions, cause and causes of action, suits, debts due, sums of money, accounts, reckonings, bonds, specialties, covenants, contracts, controversies, agreements, promises, variances, trespasses, damages, judgments, extents, executions, claims and demands whatsoever in law or equity which against said P. H. Anderson it ever had or now has, or which its successors or assigns hereafter can, shall or may have, for upon or by reason of any matter, cause or thing whatso-

[59] *White Star Mining Company of Illinois* v. *Nels O. Hultberg et. al.,* Supreme Court of Illinois, October term, 1904, No. 3912, *Brief and Arguments for Appellant,* p. 79.

ever, from the beginning of the world to the date of these presents.

In witness whereof, the said Swedish Evangelical Covenant of America has hereunto set its hand and affixed its seal by its President and Secretary, thereunto duly authorized, the 16th day of August, A. D. 1901.

By C. A. Bjork,
President.

D. Nyvall,
Secretary.[60]

[Seal of the Swedish
Evangelical Covenant of America.]

Signed, sealed and delivered in the
presence of C. Youngberg.

Anderson received the second release about August 21. Thereupon he sent his donation which probably arrived about August 31.[61] For the time being the difficulties had been settled.

---

[60] *Ibid.,* pp. 79 f.

[61] Sub-Committee Minutes, September 10, 1901. "The treasurer reported that he had received $25,000 for the school from P. H. Anderson." In the meeting held October 29, 1901, the treasurer reported the receipt of an additional $2,000 from Anderson, for the use of the mission work in China.

PART II—1902-1903

THE   ESKIMO LAWSUIT

THE ESKIMO LAWSUIT

In the opening months of 1902 K. J. Hendrickson, an Alaska missionary, began negotiations with two attorneys regarding the interests of the Eskimo boys in No. 9 Above. Constantine Uparazuck was then about twenty-one years old, and the alleged first owner of No. 8 Above. Gabriel Adams, the second Eskimo boy, who was the alleged first owner of No. 9 Above, was about eighteen years old when he died of typhoid fever, on July 18, 1900.

Hendrickson, on May 2, 1902, secured the appointment from the Probate Court of administrator of the "estate" of Gabriel Adams. Acting on behalf of Amanda Chupokaluk, the supposed heir at law, Hendrickson caused two attorneys, C. M. Thuland and T. M. Reed, to bring suit against Anderson in the name of Constantine, as well as of Amanda Chupokaluk and himself as administrator.[62]

On May 5, 1902, the attorneys for the Eskimos filed their bill of complaint in the United States District Court of Alaska, Second Division, at Nome. The allegations made by the plaintiffs were as follows: that Eric O. Lindblom located and staked No. 8 Above for Constantine and No. 9 Above for Gabriel; that Anderson caused G. W. Price to relocate No. 8 and No. 9; that Price kept No. 8 himself and transferred No. 9 to Anderson to hold in trust for Constantine and Gabriel; that Anderson had extracted $400,000 from his claim, but had given Hendrickson only $400 for Constantine, and refused to carry out his trust. Wherefore, the plaintiffs prayed that No. 9 Above be declared to be held by Anderson as a trustee for the plaintiffs, that Anderson be required to account for and pay over all proceeds from the mine, that a receiver be appointed, that the trust be abrogated in favor of Constantine and the estate of Gabriel, that an injunction be issued, and that further relief be given.[63]

[62] Amanda Chupokaluk was a sister of Gabriel Adams, the deceased Eskimo boy.

[63] *Abstract of Record,* pp. 488-491.

During the summer of 1902 Anderson was not in Alaska. But his friend and representative, Dr. Claes W. Johnson, was in Alaska as the manager of No. 9 Above. On behalf of the White Star Mining Company of California, a corporation organized by Anderson to conduct his mining operations, Dr. Johnson entered his appearance into the lawsuit as intervenor. Through Anderson's lawyers, C. S. Johnson, Ira Orton, and A. J. Daly, the White Star Mining Company denied the basic allegations of the plaintiffs and asserted the sole and absolute ownership of Anderson and the company to which he had conveyed his interests.[64]

Before the issues were joined in court, the lawyers on both sides evidently agreed upon a settlement. About the first part of August, Dr. A. N. Kittilsen and Amanda Chupokaluk from Unalakleet, Constantine and Hendrickson from Cheenik, together with four lawyers, met at the office of Attorney Johnson in Nome. With the aid of Alice Omegitjoak, an interpreter from Unalakleet, the plaintiffs discussed the terms of a settlement. As a result of this conference, an out-of-court settlement was agreed upon, and the attorneys of the plaintiffs agreed that judgment be entered in favor of the defendants.[65]

Upon motion for judgment, therefore, the cause was terminated by the following judgment:

Uparazuck, *et al.*
vs.
Anderson and White Star } *Judgment*
Mining Company.

This cause coming on upon motion for a judgment, and the parties being represented by counsel, and it appearing satisfactorily to the court that said Constantine Uparazuck and K. Hendrickson, administrator, etc. and said estate of Gabriel Adams, deceased, have no lawful or valid claim or demands, nor have either of them, of any kind or nature whatsoever against said P. H. Anderson or said intervenor, and that neither they nor either of them

64 *Ibid.*, pp. 491-495.
65 *White Star Mining Company of Illinois* v. *Nels O. Hultberg et. al.,* Supreme Court of Illinois, December Term, 1905, No. 3912, *Reply for Appellant,* pp. 21 f.

have any interest whatsoever in the gold dust heretofore extracted from said No. 9.

It is hereby ordered, adjudged and decreed that the deed from R. L. Price to said defendant, P. H. Anderson, of said No. 9, made on November 17, 1898, was the full and absolute deed of said property and no trust in said property in favor of said Constantine, or the estate of said Gabriel, was ever declared by said R. L. Price or said P. H. Anderson, or by any one in their behalf.

It is further ordered, adjudged and decreed by the court that said Constantine Uparazuck, K. Hendrickson, or the estate of said Gabriel Adams, deceased, do not now have, nor did they or either of them have any estate, right, title or interest in and to said mining claim or any part thereof, and that no trust exists now or ever did exist in favor of said Constantine, or said Gabriel, or the estate of Gabriel.

It is further ordered, adjudged, and decreed that said Constantine, Gabriel or the estate of Gabriel are not now entitled and never were entitled to any share or interest in the gold dust extracted from said placer mining claim, or any of the profits or the emoluments of the same.

That each and every of the allegations of the complaint, by which it is attempted to erect a trust are hereby declared to be not true.

Done in open court in Nome, Alaska, this 10th day of August, 1902.

Alfred S. Moore,
United States District Judge.[66]

Uparazuck, *et al.*
vs. } Confession of Judgment.
P. H. Anderson

Said plaintiff, Constantine Uparazuck, and said plaintiff, K. Hendrickson, administrator, etc., Amanda Chupokaluk, for good and valuable consideration, do by these presents on behalf of themselves and the estate of Gabriel Adams, deceased, confess and say that they and said estate have no lawful or valid claims or demands of any kind or nature against said defendant, P. H. Anderson,

[66] *Abstract of Record*, pp. 497 f.

and they, and said estate have no interest whatever in gold extracted or to be extracted from said No. 9, or in any profits thereof which have heretofore accrued, or shall hereafter accrue to either said Anderson or his grantees.

And they do by these presents confess and declare that they have not now and never did have any interest, either legal or equitable in said No. 9 and they confess and declare said mining company is the full and absolute owner of the legal and equitable estate of said undivided seven-eighths interest.

And said Constantine Uparazuck and K. Hendrickson, administrator, and Amanda Chupokaluk, do confess judgments in favor of said defendant, P. H. Anderson, and that a decree of this court be made and entered that they take nothing from said P. H. Anderson, and that said mining company be decreed to be the full and absolute owner of an undivided seven-eighths in said No. 9.

Warrant of attorney
(signed) Aug. 12, 1902.

> Constantine Uparazuck, (Seal),
> K. Hendrickson, Administrator, etc., (Seal),
> Amanda Chupokaluk, her (Seal),
> > > > Plaintiffs.

In presence of:
A. N. Kittilsen,
Alice Omegitjoak.

Said confession of judgment above set forth has been read by us, the attorneys of said plaintiff, before the same was signed by them, and we do hereby agree and consent that judgment be entered in favor of P. H. Anderson and the White Star Mining Co., a corporation, as hereinbefore provided.

Witness our hands and seals this 12th day of August, A. D. 1902.

> C. M. Thuland and
> T. M. Reed,
> Attorneys for the above named plaintiffs.[67]

Certificate of acknowledgment before notary.

[67] *Ibid.*, pp. 495 f.

Results of a cleanup.

Nome in 1900.

The terms of the out-of-court settlement were as follows: Constantine and Gabriel's heir were to receive $25,000, payable at the rate of $500 to each one for twenty-five years. The plaintiffs received a cash payment of $13,000, which was then paid to the attorneys for legal fees. In addition, Constantine was promised a schooner, of at least $1,500 value, to be delivered by 1903. Thus, by this settlement Anderson paid $39,500 to clear his title to No. 9 Above. In addition, his own lawyers charged a fee of $35,000. This fee was considered exhorbitant, and was not paid. Thereupon, Anderson's lawyers secured a judgment against No. 9 Above. In the summer of 1903, when the threat was made of putting No. 9 Above up for sale by the U. S. Marshal, the matter was compromised by the payment of $17,500. Hence, the total settlement cost approximated $57,000, of which over half went to the lawyers.[68]

The Gathering Storm

The settlement with the Covenant in August, 1901, and the settlement of the lawsuit with the Eskimos in August, 1902, had left Anderson in acknowledged possession of No. 9 Above. Legally, he had been the absolute possessor since November 17, 1898, and after August, 1902, he had cleared himself of counter claims. It would seem, therefore, that his troubles were finally ended.

But appearances are proverbially deceptive. Anderson's troubles theoretically were over, but actually they were just beginning. During the summer of 1902, the Covenant officials had received from O. P. Anderson a letter charging P. H. Anderson with alleged indiscreet conduct toward an Eskimo girl while serving as a missionary at Golovnin Bay, and in October Bjork had received a letter from Hultberg, who preferred further charges of misconduct.[69] These charges of Hultberg and O. P. Anderson were discussed in the meeting of the sub-committee of November 3, and consequently, it was decided to summon P. H. Anderson. On November 11, the sub-com-

68 MS. Record, pp. 140, 168 f.

69 Sub-Committee Minutes, July 1, 1902, August 19, September 2 and November 3.

mittee held a meeting with Anderson to discuss the charges against him. In the absence of Bjork, Mellander was elected chairman, and he reviewed the purpose of the meeting. Anderson said he was not answerable to the committee, but agreed to meet with certain members. The committee accepted the proposition with the reservation that it would meet again to consider further action. On November 14, Anderson met privately with Nyvall and Bjork, with whom he discussed the charges of imprudent conduct in Alaska. On November 18, he appeared a second time before the sub-committee, which arrived at the following conclusions:

1. Anderson should deposit $15,000, for the use of the Eskimo girl, the money being subject to the control of the Covenant committee.
2. Anderson should secure Hultberg's forgiveness and settle with him in such manner as he could.
3. Anderson should willingly give up as a matter of conscience that which he knew did not belong to him, and that the release, which he had requested of the Covenant, should not stand in the way.[70]

Anderson was reported to have given oral acquiescence on the first two points, but not on the significant—and crucial—third point. A lively discussion followed, the spirit of which may be appreciated in the colorful and confused testimony of Petterson:

> Then the third point: Pastor Bjork say to him that he should give up all the money what he have in his possession, was belong to him—'Give it up to the Mission, or whoever it was belonged; if he thought it belonged to all the Missions, give it to the Mission it did belong to.'
>
> Anderson said, 'I know, my God, so that I have not anything but belongs to me.' Then Anderson said he had nothing, and he got kind of hard then, you know. Everything belonged to him what he got. He didn't want to do anything about the third question. We sat there for a little while and we talked a good deal about such and such a thing, and asked him that everything is gone if we don't have our hearts clear and ready to meet God. Well, we are

---

70 *Ibid.,* November 18, 1902. See also MS. Record, pp. 1003 f.

lost. We all said that, spoke to Anderson and Anderson
said so. Anderson had all the money and the devil got in
him, and he couldn't get rid of the devil and the money,
and that is the way I felt and spoke in that way a good
many times. I mean money in No. 9. He wrote a letter
and mentioned my name and thought he would get me on
the bad side in the Committee and in society. I went down
and say to him about the money question, and so I told
him what Brynteson told me, and I don't see why Brynteson should tell me when I didn't know anything about it,
that the claim No. 9 was staked, restaked of Price, because he got No. 8, and so he staked No. 9, and sold the
No. 9 to Anderson as the foreman for the Mission, out
there for the Mission. I don't see why Brynteson should
tell me that: I haven't been up in Alaska. I don't know
nothing about it any more than other people.[71]

Secretary Nyvall was commissioned to write to Hultberg and
to the missionaries in Alaska regarding the outcome of the
meeting.

When the sub-committee met on December 2, Nyvall read
a letter wherein Hultberg replied to Nyvall's letter. Hultberg
evidently asserted the Covenant's ownership of No. 9, since it
was decided to ask Hultberg to secure from G. W. Price an
affidavit regarding the staking of No. 9. It was further decided
to send to Anderson the three conditions made on November
18 and to request an answer in good time before the semi-
annual meeting on January 30, 1903.[72]

Whether Anderson made a formal reply to these conditions
is not apparent. But what is evident is that Anderson anticipated further trouble in No. 9. This anticipation, together
with the charges levelled against him, seemingly precipitated
a decision which he had long meditated.

Since the fall of 1900, Anderson had not been to Alaska.
His brother managed No. 9 in 1901 and Dr. Claes W. Johnson managed it in 1902. Because of Anderson's long friend-

---

[71] *Abstract of Record,* pp. 253, 254, 265.

[72] Sub-Committee Minutes, December 2, 1902. It is highly improbable that
Hultberg ever secured any such affidavit, since Price testified in 1904, on
behalf of Anderson, before the board of arbitrators. This testimony is in
MS. Record, pp. 1670 ff.

ship with Dr. Johnson, because of their common interest in a hospital building, and because of Dr. Johnson's managership of No. 9 in 1902, it is easily conceivable that Anderson had considered transferring his holdings to Dr. Johnson—apart from the difficulties with the sub-committee. These difficulties conceivably hastened the decision.[73]

In the first week of December, 1902, Anderson and Dr. Johnson discussed the plan of transferring the ownership of Anderson's properties. The discussions were continued at Joplin, Missouri, about December 15, and on January 3, 1903, the transaction was completed in Chicago.[74] The following agreement indicates the terms.

Chicago, Illinois,
January 3, 1903.

For and in consideration of the premises hereinafter set forth the undersigned promises to pay P. H. Anderson the sum of one hundred thousand dollars, without interest, to be paid at Chicago, Illinois, only out of the income to the White Star Mining Company of California, out of its property, to wit: No. 9 Above Discovery, Anvil Creek; No. 2 Above Discovery, Anvil Creek; No. 1 Above Francisco, Rock Creek; No. 7 Below, on Dry Creek—all in Cape Nome Mining District, Alaska; No. 6 Above, Melsing Creek, and No. 7 Above on Ophir Creek, in Council City District in Alaska.

It is understood that such payment is to be made out of such income after the deduction of all the operating or working expenses of such properties, including in such expenses a sum not exceeding five thousand ($5,000), which is to be allowed to the undersigned for his personal use, or, in other words, for managing expenses; and also including in such expenses any and all costs and expenditures in defending the title to said properties or in settling claims against the title to said properties.

It is understood and agreed that the consideration for the aforesaid promises to pay is the transfer to the undersigned by said P. H. Anderson of all the capital stock of

---

[73] Anderson's testimony indicates another possible reason: "I was tired of Alaska and thought I could retire" (MS. Record, p. 143).

[74] *Abstract of Record*, pp. 474-476.

said White Star Mining Company, namely five hundred thousand shares, excepting, however, not more than three of said shares.

Claes W. Johnson.[75]

Accepted: P. H. Anderson.

By this arrangement Dr. Johnson was the possessor of 499,997 shares of stock in the White Star Mining Company of California. In the spring of 1903 Dr. Johnson decided to establish in his own state of Illinois a corporation known as the White Star Mining Company of Illinois. On April 21, 1903, the secretary of state issued a commission to Dr. Claes W. Johnson, Nils F. Olson, and Adolph Bernard. The capital stock was $25,000, the number of shares 2,500, and the par value $10. Dr. Johnson held 2,480 shares, Adolph Bernard 10, and Axel Chytraus 10 shares. On May 2, the commissioners convened the stockholders in the office of Deneen and Hamill, organized the company by making Dr. Johnson president and director, Adolph Bernard, secretary and director, and Axel Chytraus, director.[76] On May 4, the final certificate of incorporation was issued by the secretary of state. Two weeks later, on May 19, 1903, the White Star Mining Company of Illinois purchased the White Star Mining Company of California.[77]

The Storm Breaks

On January 30-31, 1903, the semi-annual meeting of the executive committee was held at the Ravenswood Covenant Church. During the morning session of the second day's meeting, Hultberg was present and asked for a private session with the executive committee. His request was granted and the meeting was held immediately. Hultberg presented his charges against Anderson, stated his views on the Covenant's ownership of No. 9 Above, and asked for the appointment of a com-

---

[75] *Ibid.,* p. 477.

[76] *Ibid.,* pp. 212, 213, 360. Adolph Bernard was the brother of Dr. Johnson.

[77] *Claes W. Johnson* v. *Nels O. Hultberg et. al.,* Supreme Court of the United States, October Term, 1906, No. 647, *Transcript of Record,* p. 102. See also *Nels O. Hultberg and Swedish Evangelical Mission Covenant of America* v. *Peter H. Anderson et al.,* Supreme Court of Illinois, June Term, 1911, No. 7712, *Brief and Argument for Plaintiffs in Error,* p. 36.

mittee of three to settle, amicably if possible, with Anderson, and urged the full executive committee to meet again the following week to consider the report of the special committee. In case no settlement could be made, the executive committee would then decide upon the next steps. In response to this request, the executive committee appointed C. G. Petterson, C. A. Youngquist, and S. A. Matson to work with Hultberg.[78]

It was not feasible for the executive committee to meet on February 6, but the sub-committee held a meeting on February 26, 1903, to which Hultberg and his attorney, N. Soderberg,[79] were invited. Soderberg presented a series of resolutions and propositions, as follows:

1. Hultberg had been the Covenant missionary in Alaska.
2. Hultberg had the right to take out his salary in goods which had been sent to the mission.
3. Hultberg owned by right $1,000 worth of goods which were at Golovnin Bay in June, 1898. Also, he owned personally about $400 deposited by A. E. Karlson with the North American Transportation and Trading Company at St. Michael.
4. A quit-claim deed to No. 9 should be given by the Covenant to Hultberg.
5. An assignment of No. 9 should be given to Hultberg for five years, on condition that he receive two-thirds of the net income.
6. Hultberg should take over the Covenant's claim upon Eric O. Lindblom.

On the first three resolutions there was no action taken, but the sub-committee probably agreed. On point four, the sub-committee said it had no such right and referred the matter to the annual meeting. On point five, the matter was referred to the executive committee, scheduled to meet in five days. On point six, several of the members approved but referred the decision to the executive committee. At this same meeting the

---

78 Sub-Committee Minutes, January 31, 1903. Actually, these are the minutes of the full executive committee.

79 N. Soderberg is referred to as Judge Soderberg. In the records he is associated both with Carson City, Nevada, and California. Probably he came to California from Nevada.

sub-committee decided to give Soderberg copies of the Covenant's incorporation papers, its by-laws, and copies of letters necessary for an investigation.[80]

On March 3, the entire executive committee assembled at North Park College for one of the most momentous meetings of its history. Matson gave a resumé of the preceding meeting for the benefit of Sundberg, Carlson, and Wallblom, who had not been present. Then the committee discussed the propositions which had been presented by Soderberg and referred by the sub-committee. The sharp disagreements, the personal predilections, and the arguments on both sides of the question can be best appreciated by a summary of the individual viewpoints.[81]

Those who were most sympathetic with Hultberg were Bjork, Mellander, and Petterson.[82] Bjork reviewed his talk with Judge Chytraus about the release, and said that both sides understood that the money given had been a donation and not a payment of an indebtedness. He said that he had sent the release because Anderson demanded it, and he admitted that Anderson's reason for insisting on the release was "so that nothing would come thereafter." Nevertheless, Bjork contended that the release had no significance. Since Hultberg would start a lawsuit no matter what the Covenant did, and since it was impossible therefore to avoid a lawsuit, Bjork said the committee should grant Hultberg's request.

Mellander sought to justify Hultberg's actions. If Hultberg had acted unwisely, it was so because he had acted hastily. If Hultberg did not have kindly feelings toward the Covenant, it was because he considered himself ill-treated by the executive committee. If Hultberg believed that there was a conspiracy against him, that was so because he thought that the Covenant's officials had done wrong toward him. After all, Mellander reminded his colleagues, we have a responsibility

---

[80] Sub-Committee Minutes, February 26, 1903.

[81] Sub-Committee Minutes, March 3, 1903. Again, it should be noted, these minutes are for the full executive committee.

[82] President Bjork, one would expect, felt some apprehension because of having signed the release. Mellander and Petterson, militant and aggressive in their opposition to Anderson, were the two men most responsible for the decisions made in 1903.

for the wrong done Hultberg. He is an honourable man. All he wants is to rent No. 9. Even if we don't make a dollar, we have contributed to the process of justice. We should protect ourselves by a contract whereby Hultberg takes all the responsibility and assumes all the costs. We have nothing to lose.[83]

Petterson said that the committee should grant all of Hultberg's requests and help him in every respect. He contended, somewhat inconsistently, that Hultberg had decided to initiate a lawsuit on behalf of the Covenant because he felt more kindly now toward the denomination than formerly. If Hultberg had become rich, Petterson said, we don't know how he would have acted, but we do know that he is not guilty of any wrong. Since he is willing to give the Covenant whatever portion it stipulates, we can do no wrong in helping him secure for us what we have lost. The release does not hinder us at all, he asserted.[84]

Among those who disagreed with the views expressed was Aaron Carlson. He pointed out that the committee was inconsistent. It was not right to give Anderson a release and then take up the matter again. If the committee members felt that at one time they had been intimidated, then let them remain intimidated. If the executive committee previously did not feel that it had a strong enough right to go to law, then it should not now help others to initiate a lawsuit. So far as the release was concerned, Carlson thought that it was illegal because the executive committee could not give away Covenant property. Nevertheless, the committee should not refuse to acknowledge what it had already decided on the matter of the release. Let the committee proceed carefully, do nothing precipitously, but refer the matters to the judgment of the annual meeting.[85]

[83] Mellander was so strongly influenced by the moral charges against Anderson that he minimized legal considerations. For the lawyers, the moral charges against Anderson were considered irrelevant and immaterial, even if they could be proved.

[84] Petterson had been the one to make the motion on April 1, 1901, to accept Anderson's money as a voluntary donation. He had become convinced, however, that No. 9 Above did not belong to Anderson. His attitude is seen in his testimony: "I feel very intensely on this subject—I have been worked up on this matter since 1899. . . . I was in to go for the man, and was down to a lawyer [O. C. Peterson?] and spoke about it, and he told me I should do so *(Abstract of Record,* pp. 256, 260).

[85] Sub-Committee Minutes, March 3, 1903.

Although S. A. Matson thought that No. 9 belonged to the Covenant, he also believed that Hultberg was motivated more by a burning desire for vengeance than by any love for the Covenant. Hultberg on many occasions had shown himself to be impetuous and incautious. He may mean well, but he is not alone; he is certainly dependent on other people's judgment. Furthermore, since these other people are unknown to us, it is hazardous to support them in a lawsuit on our behalf. A lawsuit will embroil innocent people. Moreover, with canny foresight, in the light of subsequent litigation, Matson predicted that even if the Covenant should obtain $75,000, as Soderberg had temptingly intimated, this case might drag on in the courts for years and years.[86]

Like Bjork, Nyvall had a special interest in the debate because he had signed the release. He reviewed the developments leading up to the release. When the semi-annual meeting was held in February, 1901, the executive committee had demanded a larger sum than had been offered. Upon Anderson's refusal to comply with this demand, it was decided—on the motion of Petterson—that Anderson's gift be accepted on his own terms. When Anderson asked for a release, Nyvall had sought to dissuade him, but Anderson insisted on the release. Thus, matters stood when the executive committee at Duluth recommended the acceptance of the gift—which naturally included Anderson's conditions. The annual meeting accepted the gift made under those conditions. The release was sent to Anderson twice, after a conference with Judge Chytraus. The entire executive committee was responsible for the handling of this matter.

Nyvall pointed out that Hultberg had intended to include the Covenant as a defendant in a lawsuit in case the denomination refused to help him against his enemies. Hultberg had even insinuated that the Covenant was a part of the conspiracy against him. It was wrong to engage in a lawsuit after Anderson had been given a release. Also, he agreed with Matson that one could not see the end of litigation once begun, and that persons like Brynteson and missionary Karlson would be

[86] Matson's prediction came true. Litigation developed the following year and continued for fifteen years.

implicated. Nyvall concluded by saying that he could not vote on any of the propositions made by Hultberg and his lawyer. The only proposition he would entertain would be that of referring the matter to the annual meeting. On any other proposal, he would abstain from taking any responsibility by voting.[87]

Sundberg gave it as his opinion that No. 9 had been intended for the mission, but Anderon had so arranged that he was the legal owner. Therefore the Covenant had no grounds for going to court and had no witnesses strong enough to support a lawsuit. Sundberg acknowledged that he had approved the process leading to the giving of the release. Therefore, Anderson should be considered the legal owner. The only thing that the Covenant would gain as compensation for the lawsuit would be shame and ignominy. Before the bar of public opinion, the executive committee would appear as impostors and swindlers.[88]

Wallblom said that he agreed with the views of Aaron Carlson. Wallblom added that the Covenant had nothing to gain by helping Hultberg in this lawsuit inasmuch as Hultberg himself had shown very little interest for the Covenant. With cool and embarrassing logic, Wallblom asserted that if president Bjork and secretary Nyvall had acted against the committee's will, they should be discharged, indicted, and arrested; but, if they had acted in accordance with the committee's will, then their signatures must stand as the decision of the entire committee. Let the committee take no responsibility for Hultberg's requests, but rather refer them to the annual meeting.[89]

The upshot of the heated and acrimonious debate held during the long afternoon was a decision to do nothing until a meeting had been held with Hultberg and Soderberg.

On the evening of March 3, when the executive committee

[87] *Ibid.* Nyvall's views, it seems to me, were objective and impartial. He was critical of Anderson, and yet he did not condemn him. He tried to see the problem without prejudice, and concluded that there was insufficient evidence to prove a trusteeship. Furthermore, he regarded the release as valid, and he deplored the resort to the courts (Nyvall MSS. and personal interviews).

[88] Sub-Committee Minutes, March 3, 1903.

[89] *Ibid.* Wallblom believed, of course, that Bjork and Nyvall had carried out the mandate of the executive committee.

assembled once more, Hultberg and N. Soderberg were present, and also the latter's son, W. F. Soderberg.

A long discussion was held on point six—that Hultberg should take over the Covenant's claim upon Eric O. Lindblom. The facts supporting this claim were these: Lindblom had arrived at Golovnin Bay, a destitute man, had signed a grubstake contract with Hultberg on July 26, 1898, to work on Hultberg's claims, No. 5 on Melsing Creek and No. 6 on Ophir Creek, both claims being in the Council City region.[90] About a month later, Hultberg encouraged Lindblom to go to Nome. Two weeks after Hultberg had left Alaska, Lindblom did go to Nome and became one of the lucky three discoverers. Hultberg believed that Lindblom had not kept his contract. Accordingly, in the fall of 1899, Hultberg initiated a lawsuit against Lindblom. On behalf of the Covenant, secretary Nyvall sent Hultberg a telegram in December, urging him to withdraw the suit. Axel Anderson, A. E. Karlson, and John Brynteson also urged him to drop the suit. Lindblom promised to pay Hultberg $3,000 and the Covenant $15,000, the latter sum evidently as compensation for provisions and housing which Lindblom had enjoyed during the winter of 1898-99 in northern Alaska. Lindblom paid Hultberg $3,000, promised orally to pay the Covenant $15,000 in 1900, paid $5,000 in 1901, and left unpaid a balance of $10,000.[91]

After prolonged discussion about Lindblom, the committee took up the proposition of leasing No. 9 to Hultberg. W. F. Soderberg reviewed the story of the staking of the claims, said that the two Eskimo claims were intended for the Covenant mission, and asserted that by the restaking Anderson was to hold No. 9 for the mission. He did admit, however, that the deed conveying No. 9 to Anderson specified closely that Anderson purchased and held No. 9 for his own use and profit.[92]

After this discussion, the executive committee met separately and arrived at three conclusions. They decided that Hult-

---

[90] The contract, which promised Hultberg one-half of the gold extracted in 1898, is printed in *Abstract of Record*, pp. 340 f.

[91] MS. Record, pp. 984, 986, 1548, 1556.

[92] The second deed of March 8, 1899, conveyed the claim to Anderson "to and for his own use and behoof forever."

berg should be given a power of attorney in order to recover the unpaid portion of the sum which Lindblom had promised. For this, Hultberg was to have 10 per cent. On the matter of No. 9, the committee decided to lease the claim to Hultberg, subject to the approval of the annual conference. Hultberg was to receive one-half of the net profits, and in return was to sign a contract releasing the Covenant from all demands and responsibility in the lawsuit. On the matter of claims against all other persons who had taken anything out of No. 9, the committee made no recommendations, but referred the question to the annual meeting.[93]

Having made these decisions, the executive committee called in Hultberg, N. Soderberg, and W. F. Soderberg, and presented their recommendations. Attorney N. Soderberg prevailed upon the committee to strike the phrase "as it may appear" from one resolution. On the decision to give Hultberg a power of attorney, Soderberg contended that by such an arrangement Hultberg became an agent who could sue Lindblom in the name of the Covenant. Thereupon, the committee decided to give Hultberg his original request—an assignment of the Covenant's claim upon Lindblom, whereby Hultberg would sue in his own name. On the most important matter of all, Soderberg pointed out that a lease would be of little value, since the Covenant would still be the owner. The committee then decided to recommend that Hultberg be given a quit-claim deed instead.[94]

Tempers must have been strained as the executive committee concluded its arduous session. Opinion was united mainly on referring decisions to the annual meeting. On other matters opinion was sharply divided. The entire problem was complicated still further when Mellander on his own initiative and responsibility appealed to public opinion in a scathing article against Anderson, published in the same month, March, 1903.[95]

When the executive committee finished its business, it as-

[93] Some of the other persons were David Johnson Elliot, George Howard, Dr. A. G. Anderson, and Dr. Claes W. Johnson, all of whom had worked on No. 9 Above as lease holders or managers.

[94] Sub-Committee Minutes, March 3, 1903.

[95] This article was published in the *Missionären*. This paper was the official Covenant organ, but the *Missions-Vännen* was the most widely read paper in 1903.

signed the sub-committee the task of working out details. One of the items which some members wished to adjust was a statement in the sub-committee minutes for August 6, 1901. In reference to the release, the secretary had written "and which the committee in Duluth in pursuance of the decision of the annual meeting [1901] decided to give him [Anderson]." The sub-committee which met on June 2, 1903, decided on the motion of Mellander that this statement was incorrect and should be stricken. It was accordingly stricken, the implication being that the release had been unauthorized.[96]

The annual conference assembled in Minneapolis on June 11, 1903, for a five-day session. Uppermost in the minds of many delegates was "the Anderson question" which had been widely discussed. The delegates were made aware of how deeply feelings had been hurt by this problem when Nyvall, after reading his secretary's report on June 11, announced that under no circumstances would he accept the secretaryship for the following year. Despite persistent efforts to persuade him, he refused to stand for re-election. Upon the proposal made to the conference by E. A. Skogsbergh, however, Nyvall did accept the commission to journey to Alaska immediately after the conference, to learn at first-hand the needs of the Alaska mission field, to counsel with the missionaries, and to make a detailed report for the next annual conference.[97]

---

[96] This action was sharply criticized later by the lawyers, who called the attention of the court "to the fraudulent misconduct of the Covenant and of Hultberg in the alteration of the records of the Covenant, with a view to destroy part of proof of the Covenant's knowledge and approval of the settlement, *made in contemplation of action against these petitioners*" [Anderson and Dr. Johnson] (See Supreme Court of Illinois, No. 3912; *White Star Mining Company of Illinois* vs. *Nels O. Hultberg et al.; Petition for Rehearing by White Star Mining Company, Peter H. Anderson and Claes W. Johnson*, p. 63. See also *ibid., Reply for Appellant, White Star Mining Company of Illinois, and Appellees, Claes W. Johnson and Peter H. Anderson, to Argument for Appellees, Nels O. Hultberg and the Swedish Evangelical Mission Covenant of America in Reply to the Petition for a Rehearing*, p. 78). Although the alteration of the minutes cannot be regarded as "fraudulent misconduct," inasmuch as the minutes were "altered" by drawing a pencil line through them, with the fact itself officially recorded in the minutes, nevertheless, the action was unfortunate. Nyvall, who had written the minutes in 1901, testified that the entry in the margin, "observe, corrections according to resolve on June 2, 1903," was not in his handwriting. Evidently the correction was a result of pressure from Hultberg's lawyers *(Abstract of Record*, p. 442).

[97] *Förbundets Nittonde Årsmöte i Minneapolis, Minnesota, 1903*, pp. 132, 137. Professor Nyvall did go to Alaska in 1903 and learned at first-hand

It was not until June 15 that question of No. 9 was taken up. The morning session was closed to all except official delegates, and F. Boring was commissioned to take down the entire discussion in shorthand. The report of the executive committee, consisting mainly of extracts from the minutes, was read and accepted. Thereupon, Mellander, speaking neither for the Covenant nor the executive committee, but only on his own responsibility, gave a detailed lengthy summary of the question of No. 9 Above. He reviewed the history of the case, explained why he had attacked Anderson publicly, defended the Covenant's ownership of the mine, and minimized the binding force of the release. Mellander's report was received with a unanimous and powerful approval.[98]

The afternoon deliberations continued in a closed session. A. Hallner, who was Hultberg's personal representative at the conference, reported on Hultberg's views and actions. Upon the request of Mellander, a committee of three was appointed to examine the documents and correspondence which substantiated his morning's speech. This committee reported that what Mellander had said was based on first-rate witnesses, not hearsay, and that these witnesses could testify before a court. The committee reported further that it exonerated Mellander from the charges levelled against him by his critics because of his article published in *Missionären.*[99]

After discussing the question of Anderson's release, the delegates took a momentous step when they appointed a committee, consisting of Hallner, Mellander, and J. J. Daniels, to consult with a reliable lawyer. Jointly, they were commissioned to draw up a resolution setting aside the release as null and void. This resolution was to be subscribed by the trustees and then to be entered in the recorder's office in Nome, Alaska.

The rest of the afternoon's session was spent in debating the same problem. S. O. Lindgren and Nils Peterson spoke on

some of the problems to be solved. In 1897 he had edited a book, *Alaska Förr och Nu* (Chicago, 1897) which revealed a deep interest in Alaska.

98 Mellander's speech probably lasted two or even three hours. He first read extracts from the minutes, on behalf of the executive committee, and then gave his review of the entire question. See *Förbundets Nittonde Årsmöte i Minneapolis, Minnesota, 1903,* p. 148.

99 *Ibid.,* p. 151.

behalf of Anderson, and C. G. Petterson and Otto Högfeldt spoke against him.[100] Probably the most objective and sensible position was taken by Nyvall, who believed that the delegates had been stampeded into a false decision by the arguments of Mellander. Nyvall believed that the moral accusations against Anderson were irrelevant to the legal question of ownership, but many of the delegates, Mellander included, inclined to the view that if a man is culpable in one situation he is at fault in another.[101]

The afternoon's session was terminated after heated discussions of the problem. Many of the delegates must have felt some forebodings as S. O. Lindgren read a letter sent from Brazil by P. H. Anderson, who threatened a lawsuit against the Covenant if Mellander's article in the *Missionären* was not retracted.[102] Before the afternoon's adjournment, it was decided to hold two special sessions throughout the evening.

During the first evening session, President Bjork gave a report on No. 9. Then J. Sällstrom, after a long preamble, proposed a resolution that Mellander be absolved of the accusations made against him for his public condemnation of Anderson in the Covenant Paper. This resolution was accepted by a standing vote of all except three of the delegates.[103] During the second session the newly elected secretary, Mellander, read those portions of the executive committee's report pertaining to the negotiations with Hultberg. Of the several recommendations made, the delegates decided (1) that Hultberg had been a faithful missionary from 1893 to 1899; (2) that it was intended that he should receive in advance a salary of $1,000 in goods; (3) that the $400 left at St. Michael by Karlson was Hultberg's own money; (4) that Hultberg is to have the right

[100] *Ibid.*, p. 150.

[101] Nyvall MSS.

[102] *Förbundets Nittonde Årsmöte i Minneapolis, Minnesota, 1903*, p. 150. Anderson sued the Covenant for $75,000 damages *(Förbundets Tjugonde Årsmöte i Paxton, Illinois, 1904*, p. 87).

[103] Sällstrom seems to have been pompous and bombastic in his utterances, and lacking in good judgment and self-control. For his unbridled remarks at the Paxton conference in 1904, he was rebuked by the conference (MSS. Minutes of the Paxton Conference Debate, pp. 81, 82 and Appendix, p. 52).

The three dissenting delegates most likely were N. Peterson, S. O. Lindgren, and D. Nyvall. The latter testified, "I didn't take any part in the fight" (MS. Record, p. 1927).

to retake what belongs to the Covenant [No. 9], with such conditions and methods as he and the executive committee shall decide. If Hultberg does not do this, then the trustees shall do so.[104]

After these decisions had been made by the conference, the trustees consulted with a lawyer, and made a stipulation, as follows:

THIS INDENTURE, made this 17th day of June, in the year of Our Lord one thousand nine hundred and three (1903) between the Swedish Evangelical Mission Covenant of America (a corporation under the laws of the State of Illinois), party of the first part, and Nels O. Hultberg, of the County of Santa Clara, and State of California, party of the second part.

WITNESSETH: That the said party of the first part, in consideration of the sum of one dollar ($1) to it in hand paid by the said party of the second part, the receipt whereof is hereby acknowledged, does hereby grant, bargain, sell, remise, release, quit-claim and convey unto the said party of the second part, his heirs and assigns forever, all the following tract or parcel of land, lying and being in the County of ...... and Territory of Alaska, described as follows, to wit:

Claim No. 9 Above, discovered on Anvil Creek in Cape Nome.

To have and to hold the above quit-claimed premises, together with all the hereditaments and appurtenances thereunto belonging or in any wise appertaining to the said party of the second part, his heirs and assigns forever.

IN TESTIMONY WHEREOF, the said party of the first part has caused these presents to be executed in its corporate name by its trustees, and its corporate seal to be hereunto affixed the day and year first above written.

The Swedish Evangelical Mission Covenant of America, by

Swan A. Matson,	Charley Wallblom,
Charles G. Petterson,	C. Aug. Youngquist,
Aaron Carlson,	Trustees.[105]

104 Sub-Committee Minutes, June 15, 1903.
105 *Abstract of Record,* p. 322.

STATE OF MINNESOTA,)
COUNTY OF HENNEPIN.) ss.

On this 17th day of June, A. D. 1903, before me, a notary public, within and for said county, personally appeared Charles G. Petterson, Aaron Carlson, Charley Wallblom, C. Aug. Youngquist, to me personally known, who, being each by me duly sworn, did say that they are the trustees of the Swedish Evangelical Mission Covenant of America, the corporation named in the foregoing instrument, that the seal affixed to said instrument is the corporate seal of said corporation, and that said instrument was signed and sealed in behalf of said corporation by authority of its Board of Trustees, and said trustees acknowledged the said instrument to be the free act and deed of said corporation.

(Also a like certificate of acknowledgement as to Swan A. Carlson, [Matson] by John P. Moran, Notary Public in Cook County, Illinois, dated June 25, 1903.)

(Also certificate of record on August 3, 1903, by T. M. Reed, recorder of deeds.)[106]

Although this indenture was made out by the trustees after consultation with a lawyer, it omitted two significant points. One was that Hultberg promised to give the Covenant one-third of what he obtained. Expressed differently, Hultberg was offered two-thirds of the net profits from No. 9 on condition that he assumed the responsibility and expense of any litigation. The trustees seemed to be more concerned with legal and financial immunity (neither of which they obtained) than with potential returns from the mining claim. The second serious omission was that the indenture said nothing about the net proceeds taken out of No. 9 *before* June 17, 1903. To correct this omission, in order to attack the $335,000 which Anderson had already obtained, the trustees found it necessary to draft a second quit-claim deed which assigned Hultberg all the gold extracted "previous and anterior to the date of said deed." This second deed, which was not drawn up until September 8, 1903, is as follows:

---

[106] *Ibid.*, p. 323. The records have the name "Carlson," but this must be a printer's error for "Matson."

KNOW ALL MEN BY THESE PRESENTS, that the Swedish Evangelical Mission Covenant of America, assignor, in consideration of the sum of one dollar, and other valuable considerations (the receipt whereof is hereby acknowledged) does hereby sell, assign, transfer and quit-claim to Nels O. Hultberg, assignee, all of the claims and demands which the said assignor now has or has had against Claes W. Johnson, White Star Mining Company (a California corporation), White Star Mining Company (an Illinois corporation), and P. H. Anderson, growing out of the said assignor's rights in and ownership of that certain placer mine and mining claim known and called No. 9 Above, on Anvil Creek, situate in the Cape Nome Mining and Recording District, in the District of Alaska; the meaning and intention of this assignment being more fully expressed as follows:

Whereas, the said assignor did, on or about the 17th day of June, 1903, convey by deed to said assignee, all the right, title and interest of said assignor in and to the said certain placer mine and mining claim known and called, "No. 9 Above on Anvil Creek," situate in the Cape Nome Mining and Recording District, in the District of Alaska, and,

Whereas, the said assignor omitted by said deed to the said assignee (executed on or about June 17, 1903, as aforesaid), to convey, assign and transfer to said assignee, all the claims and demands of the said assignor against said Claes W. Johnson, White Star Mining Company (a California corporation), White Star Mining Company (an Illinois corporation), and P. H. Anderson, of gold obtained or extracted by said parties from said mine and mining claim known and called, "No. 9 Above on Anvil Creek," situate in the Cape Nome Mining and Recording District in the District of Alaska, previous and anterior to the date of said deed;

NOW, THEREFORE, the said ASSIGNOR, by this assignment, does hereby sell, assign, transfer and set over to the said assignee all the claims and demands of said assignor against said Claes W. Johnson, White Star Mining Company (a California corporation), White Star Mining Company (an Illinois corporation), and P. H.

70

Anderson, for gold obtained or extracted by them from the certain placer mine and mining claim known and called, "No. 9 Above on Anvil Creek," situate in the Cape Nome Mining and Recording District in the District of Alaska, previous and anterior to the date of said deed so executed by said assignor to said assignee on or about June 17, 1903, as aforesaid; which said gold so extracted by said parties from said mining claim was not accounted for by said parties to said assignor; and which belonged to said assignor;

It is the meaning and intention hereof that this assignment shall relate to and be construed with and become part and parcel of said deed the same as if this assignment had been included in said deed.

And the said assignor does hereby irrevocably appoint the said assignee, its true and lawful attorney, with full power and authority in his own name and at the sole risk, cost and charge of the said assignee, his executors, administrators and assigns, to arbitrate for and to appoint arbitrators therefor, to sue for, recover and receive the said claims and demands hereby assigned, or the equivalent thereof in money or other property (said assignee to be the sole judge as to what should be deemed an equivalent), and to give good and sufficient releases for the same; and also full power and authority to appoint a substitute or substitutes for the purposes aforesaid, and such substitution from time to time at pleasure to revoke, said assignor hereby ratifying and confirming all that the said assignee, his executors, administrators or assigns or his or their substitute or substitutes shall lawfully do or cause to be done in the premises by virtue of these presents; and the said assignor hereby confirms and approves any previous acts or agreements which said assignee may have done or made, and which are not contrary to the terms of this assignment.

This instrument is executed pursuant to resolution of the said Swedish Evangelical Covenant of America, assembled in annual conference, at Minneapolis, Minnesota, on June 15, 1903.

IN WITNESS WHEREOF, we, the undersigned, as trustees of the Swedish Evangelical Mission Covenant of

America as the act of said Swedish Evangelical Mission Covenant of America, have hereunto set our hands and seals this 8th day of September, 1903.

C. G. Petterson,
President of Trustees, (Seal.)
S. A. Matson,
Secretary of Trustees, (Seal.)
C. A. Youngquist,
Aaron Carlson,
Charley Wallblom,
As Trustee for the Swedish Evangelical
Mission Covenant of America.

F. L. Palmer,
Chas. R. Wilkinson.

Certificate of acknowledgement as to Matson and Youngquist before E. B. Witwer, notary public of Cook County, Illinois, dated September 8, 1903. As to Carlson and Wallblom before F. L. Palmer, notary public of Hennepin County, Missouri, [Minnesota] dated September 10, 1903.[107]

The Arbitration Commission

During the summer of 1903, Dr. Claes W. Johnson was the manager and legal owner of No. 9 Above. When he arrived in Alaska, he found that No. 9 was subject to a lien and about to be offered for sale by the U. S. Marshal. The reason for the lien was that in 1902 Anderson's lawyers had charged the exorbitant fee of $35,000 which Anderson refused to pay. Thereupon Anderson's lawyers secured a lien on their client's property. On July 25, Dr. Johnson effected a 50 per cent settlement, paid the lawyers $17,500, and recovered his property.[108]

More trouble was in store for Dr. Johnson. About the last week in July Hultberg arrived at Nome, together with his at-

107 MS. Record, pp. 1425-1428.
108 *Abstract of Record*, pp. 475, 476, 478, and Appendix, p. 13. See also Supreme Court of Illinois, October Term, 1904, No. 3912; *White Star Mining Company of Illinois* vs. *Nels O. Hultberg et al.; Brief and Arguments for Appellant*, p. 110.

torney N. Soderberg, and W. F. Soderberg. After recording on August 3 his newly-acquired quit-claim deed in the Nome Mining District, Hultberg was in a position to give vent to his litigious mood. Through his agent, W. F. Soderberg, he caused the following notice to be served on Dr. Johnson:

Nome, Alaska,
Aug. 4, 1903.

To The White Star Mining Company, a corporation organized under the laws of the State of Illinois:

To The White Star Mining Company, a corporation organized under the laws of California: To C. W. Johnson and Peter H. Anderson, alias Peter H. Alwyn:

I hereby demand of you and each of you the immediate possession of the certain placer mining claim known as and called "No. 9 Above," on Anvil Creek, in the Cape Nome Mining District, in the District of Alaska, of which I am the owner; together with an accounting for all gold and minerals produced by or extracted from said mine since the 30th day of June, 1903.

I further demand of you that you and each of you immediately cease and desist from working upon or extracting gold or other precious metals or minerals from said claim. Mr. W. H. Soderberg has been appointed as my agent to serve upon you this demand and notice.

Nels O. Hultberg.[109]

When Dr. Johnson was served with this notice, on August 11, he faced a difficult problem. If he acquiesced in Hultberg's demand, he would have no mine. If he contested the demand, he was certain to become involved in a lawsuit. Since the trial docket of the United States District Court of Alaska, Second Division, was filled with cases awaiting trial, there was a strong likelihood of spending a long winter at Nome. Rather than face this dilemma, Dr. Johnson agreed to submit the whole question of ownership of No. 9 to an arbitration commission. Accordingly, on August 12-14, articles of agreement were drawn up and signed by both sides.

[109] *Abstract of Record,* pp. 18 f.

The following points indicate the essentials of the "special submission to arbitration," as entered into by the two parties:

1. All points of difference shall be submitted to arbitration.

2. "There shall be a full, complete, and just determination between said parties of all matters in controversy embraced herein, regardless of all technicalities, and that said adjudication shall be had upon the true merits of said controversy and according to law."

3. Each side shall select one arbitrator.

4. On January 15, 1904, these two arbitrators shall meet at the State Bank of Chicago, and with all convenient speed select the third arbitrator.

5. Each side shall deposit at least $500 for costs of arbitration. If costs exceed $1,000, each side shall advance its proportionate share. In the final award, all statutory costs and expenses shall be paid by the losing party.

6. No. 9 Above shall not be encumbered or disposed of prior to the expiration of this arbitration agreement.

7. In case Hultberg wins the award, all proceeds of No. 9 Above during 1903 shall be included in that award, but Dr. Johnson shall be allowed operating expenses, besides $9,000 for his own services.

8. The arbitrators shall hold their sessions in Chicago.

9. The arbitrators "shall be the judges of the admissibility of evidence before them in reference to said matters in controversy, and shall be liberal and not technical, in the admission of evidence, and shall administer, or cause to be administered, oaths to the witnesses who may testify before them; but their conclusions shall be based upon legal and competent evidence only.

10. The decision of the arbitrators, or of any two of them, shall be sufficient both for matters of procedure and for the final award.[110]

110 *Ibid.,* pp. 20-33.

PART III—1904

THE ARBITRATION COMMISSION OF 1904

THE ARBITRATION COMMISSION OF 1904

In accordance with the special agreement made in Alaska in August, 1903, by Hultberg and Dr. Johnson, each side appointed an arbitrator. Hultberg selected a friend of his, David F. Lane, a mining operator from Berkeley, California. Dr. Johnson, together with Anderson, selected Abram M. Pence, a lawyer who had practiced forty-two years in Chicago. These two arbitrators met at the State Bank of Chicago on January 15, 1904, and selected a third arbitrator, Hiram T. Gilbert, another lawyer, who had practiced in Chicago for twenty-nine years.

The formal sessions of the arbitrators began on February 20, 1904, and hearings were held until March 18.[1] During these four weeks the witnesses on behalf of Hultberg testified first, and then those for Anderson. Most of the sessions were held in the late afternoons and evenings. Almost all of the evidence was heard in the office of arbitrator Pence, but one or two sessions were held in the chambers of Judge Chytraus, and oral arguments of counsel were given in the office of arbitrator Gilbert. A stenographer took down all the testimony in shorthand, transcribed it as the hearings progressed, and supplied copies to each of the arbitrators.[2]

The lawyers who appeared on behalf of Hultberg were Nils Soderberg, a former judge from Carson City, Nevada; Frank J. Quinn, an attorney from Peoria, Illinois; and Harris F. Williams, a Chicago lawyer who served the Covenant for many years. For the side of Anderson and Dr. Johnson, Judge Axel

---

[1] All the sessions were in Chicago, Illinois.

[2] The transcribed record has been my main source for the story of the arbitration commission. The record consists of 2667 pages of testimony and exhibits, besides briefs, petitions, and abstracts. This material, referred to as MS. Record, is filed in the office of the clerk of the court, Supreme Court of Illinois, at Springfield, under case No. 7712, Vault No. 32,924.

Chytraus of the Superior Court of Cook County was the sole counsel. He had advised the Covenant in 1900-01, but in 1903 had become one of the shareholders in the newly organized White Star Mining Company of Illinois, a company which held the Alaskan properties of Anderson.[3]

At the first meeting on February 20, the arbitrators and counsel agreed upon the general procedure. They also agreed that the salary of the arbitrators should be $50 each per day of approximately six hours. In keeping with the special agreement, it was understood that the arbitrators should be the judges of the admissibility of evidence and that they should be liberal rather than technical in deciding. It was further understood, however, that their conclusions should be based on legal and competent evidence only.[4]

Evidence on Behalf of Hultberg

The first witness was A. E. Karlson. He spoke of his work as a tailor in Sweden, his arrival in the United States in 1886, and his departure for Alaska in 1887. After discussing his activities for the next eleven years at Unalakleet, including his acquisition of gold claims, Karlson testified that in November, 1898, Brynteson had just come from Nome. During his stay at Unalakleet, Brynteson stated that originally No. 8 and No. 9 had been staked for the Eskimo boys. Karlson testified further that when he himself stopped at Cheenik in February, 1899, Anderson had related that No. 9 had been restaked because it was believed that Eskimo boys could not hold claims.

Then Karlson told of a discussion he had overheard between Hultberg and Anderson. In the summer of 1899 all

---

[3] Judge Chytraus was sharply criticized by C. G. Petterson when the latter testified on February 26. Petterson told the Judge that he couldn't be a good friend to an enemy. He accused Chytraus of serving the Covenant and then of deserting to Anderson because there was more money on that side (MS. Record, pp. 1036 f.). In defense of Chytraus, it should be said that he gave his services to the Covenant without compensation. Regarding the other insinuation, it needs to be said that attorney John J. Healy, who worked for years with Chytraus, made the statement to the writer that Chytraus charged very little compensation for his services.

[4] The entire special arbitration agreement is printed in *Abstract of Record,* pp. 20-33.

three men were walking from Anvil Creek over the tundra to Nome. Hultberg insisted that No. 9 belonged to the Covenant, that the first gold taken from the mine should be used to ease the Covenant's debt of $15,000, and that Anderson as superintendent should not charge more than $15 a day for his work. Anderson argued that he should be allowed $20 a day because of the responsibilities involved. Anderson also insisted on the right of specifying for what purposes the money would be used. There was some argument at this time about the ownership of No. 9. Hultberg pressed the Covenant's claim, but later in the year, Karlson admitted, Anderson asserted his own individual ownership.

Karlson's testimony was significant, since he had been a contemporary observer, but on several points his answers were inadequate. He was unable to make any certain statement about Brynteson's real attitude. While asserting that Anderson implied that the Covenant owned the mine, he testified that Anderson claimed to be the owner. He was sometimes misguided by leading questions from the interrogators, and he became irritated at times by acute questioning during the cross-examination. He bluntly refused to answer some questions, and excused himself by saying that ever since an attack of typhoid fever his memory was faulty.[5]

David Johnson Elliott said that he first met Anderson in the summer of 1899, at which time Anderson was making plans to open up No. 9 for the Covenant. He did not claim that he owned the mine himself. When Hultberg suggested that Anderson give Elliott a lease on a part of No. 9, he contended that this mine was a mission claim and that Elliott had a prior right to a lease because he had been a missionary from 1891 to 1896. Elliott expected to obtain a lease of one-half the claim with 50 per cent of the proceeds, but instead was given a lease of one-fourth at 33⅓ per cent. When the possibility developed of

---

[5] Karlson had good reason for pleading weariness. It happened that he testified on February 22—Washington's birthday—when it was possible for the arbitrators to hold session the entire day. After an all-day grilling, he was naturally fatigued. His testimony covered 149 pages (MS. Record, pp. 651-799).

losing his claim at the hands of jumpers, Anderson gave Elliott a second lease for one-half the claim at 50 per cent, with the verbal instructions that if Anderson lost the claim Elliott could use the second lease. If Anderson won the litigation, Elliott would tear up the second lease.[6]

Under questioning, Elliott admitted that Anderson accused him of conducting operations in an unminerlike fashion. He further admitted that there had been troubles between them and that Anderson had sued him. Further embarrassed in the cross-examination, Elliott admitted that he had mismanaged funds amounting to more than $30,000 which belonged to the Pioneer Mining Company. While denying that he had embezzled the money, he confessed to negligence, carelessness, and unauthorized actions.[7]

Elliott testified repeatedly that Anderson was a trustee for the Eskimo boys and the denomination. The difficulty was that Elliott was so glib and so certain, that his testimony became almost worthless. His prejudices and conclusions were proffered as evidence, and his bias injected itself insidiously into conversation which he "remembered." Unfortunately, he did not remember what he had said to a newspaper reporter in 1899, nor did he realize that his statements made in 1899 flatly contradicted what he said in 1904.

When the first newspaper was established in Nome during the fall of 1899, Elliott was interviewed on the story of the discovery and staking of the Cape Nome Mining District. He told the story of the discovery as he had heard it from the original discoverers. He further asserted that No. 9 Above belonged to Anderson, not as a trustee, but as absolute owner. This interview, published in 1899 right after the conclusion of the first mining season, before his personal troubles with

---

[6] *Abstract of Record,* pp. 238 f.

[7] David Johnson Elliott came to Unalakleet in 1891 at the age of 19. He served until 1896 as a missionary, then returned home in 1896, resigned in 1897, and returned to Alaska as a miner in 1899. After obtaining a lease with George T. Howard on the lower one-fourth of No. 9 in 1899 (330 x 660 feet), he was forced to give up his one-eighth interest in 1900 when he was found guilty of mismanagement.

Anderson and the Pioneer Mining Company, and before the beginning of troubles with the denomination, is sufficient to nullify his later statements.[8] Moreover, it was easy for the cross-examination to show that because Elliott was unfriendly to Anderson he was biased in his testimony.

The testimony of Charles G. Petterson is colorful and confused.[9] It is significant, nevertheless, because Petterson was one of the most aggressive of all the opponents of Anderson. The most important parts of his testimony relate to his conversations with Brynteson and Lindblom, and to his own attitudes.

Peterson claimed that Brynteson had said that No. 9 belonged to the denomination. When asked if he would be willing to present his views before the officials of the denomination, Brynteson acquiesced. But when Brynteson appeared before the officials, he agreed with Anderson's claims.

Peterson further alleged that Lindblom had said: "Why don't you go for Mr. Anderson? He has got your claim and he has got plenty of money there, and he took out plenty of money. Go for him. He got it." This statement of Lindblom, however, must be considered in its setting. Lindblom had promised to give $15,000 to the denomination, had donated $5,000 but had left the balance unpaid. When he was sued by Hultberg, Lindblom lost the desire to aid the Covenant. It is understandable, therefore, that Lindblom should seek to "pass the buck" to Anderson.

Petterson's testimony is important for one other reason— the revelation of his own attitudes. He said: "My idea was that Anderson was our man, and he should make reports for his

8 See the Nome *News,* May 26, 1900, p. 3, and September 19, 1900, p. 4; see also the Nome *Gold Digger,* October 25, 1899, p. 1. The *News* was a weekly, first issued on October 9. The *Gold Digger,* also a weekly, made its initial appearance on October 25. Unfortunately, these newspapers are not available in any of our main libraries. I have used the only files available— those of the Alaska Territorial Library and Museum in Juneau.

9 It is also blunt and amusing. When Petterson testified on February 26, at least five lawyers were present. On one point Petterson retorted: "We are not people, you know, that take things like lawyers do, just by the law. We have got to have a little heart about things, you know. We know there is a God and we have to answer to him also." A wry smile probably came over Judge Chytraus' face as he quipped: "Those lawyers like the two sitting over there." In self defense, Judge Soderberg queried: "You are looking at Judge Chytraus?" (MS. Record, p. 1008).

work out there, either mission work or money affairs or any other kind. On that account we made a claim. We did not send him as a gold miner, but sent him out as a missionary, but he took the time and found gold also. He took our time, and—well, whatever it is up in Alaska that belongs to the Mission—belongs to us."[10]

Axel Mellander's testimony is especially interesting because he was the most outspoken person in denouncing Anderson. Under questioning, Mellander testified of various meetings of the executive committee, beginning in December, 1899. Mellander revealed that Hultberg and Karlson were the two main sources of the reports that No. 9 belonged to the Covenant.[11] He stated that right from the beginning Anderson claimed to be the owner of No. 9. Mellander himself admitted his frank opposition to Anderson because of his conviction that the latter had defrauded the denomination. In telling of the discussions with Brynteson, Mellander related that Brynteson said that originally the claims No. 8 and No. 9 belonged to the Eskimo boys, that in the restaking Price got No. 8 as pay for restaking the claims, and that No. 9 belonged to the Eskimo boys, but since they had been cared for by the missionaries, the denomination should receive a greater amount than it had received. Mellander also testified of his having spoken at the home of C. R. Carlson in Lindsborg, Kansas, about No. 9 and of his having published an article in the March, 1903, issue of *Missionären*.[12]

Aaron Carlson, trustee of the Covenant, confessed that he had been a "very strong advocate on the side against Mr. Anderson." When the executive committee "got scared by Ander-

---

[10] Supreme Court of Illinois, December Term 1905, No. 3912, White Star Mining Company of Illinois v. Nels O. Hultberg *et al.*, *Reply for Appellant*, pp. 56 f. See also *Abstract of Record*, pp. 251, 252, 254, 257.

[11] It should be noted that Mellander felt that these men were competent witnesses. Furthermore, Mellander had a special friendship with Karlson, with whom he had traveled through Palestine in 1901 at Karlson's expense. Nevertheless, Mellander might have had reason to question the complete reliability of the reports, since neither Hultberg nor Karlson was present at either the September or October staking. I believe that Karlson was more objective and reliable than Hultberg.

[12] MS. Record, pp. 1143-1245. See especially p. 1174, where Mellander makes a very strong attack on Anderson's morality and misconduct.

son and voted that they should receive the $25,000 as a dona-
tion," he disapproved of that vote. He weakened the significance
of his testimony when he admitted: "I have got all my information at second hand, to a certain extent." Some of his information had been tardily obtained, as seen in his surprising statement that he did not hear about the release until 1903—some
eighteen months after it had been granted.[13]

C. A. Bjork, president of the Covenant, told of his consultation with Judge Chytraus regarding Anderson's request for
a release. After discussing the matter, Bjork concluded that
the release was not of any great importance and that no harm
would be done by signing the instrument which Anderson had
sent. Bjork stated: "The secretary [Nyvall] thought Anderson
would waive a release, and we didn't know what he would do
before we got an answer from him. Before we got the answer
we reported to the conference at Duluth. We reported that Anderson would donate the money, and we accepted the donation
in Duluth before we received the money, and before we received the answer about the release." Bjork further testified
that as late as February, 1903, "nobody said that the Covenant
had any claim upon Anderson as a matter of right."[14]

C. A. Youngquist, trustee and treasurer of the Covenant,
spoke of his meeting with Anderson. Youngquist said that in
various committee meetings Anderson always maintained his
ownership of No. 9 by virtue of his purchase from Price.
Questioned about contributions made by Anderson to him as
treasurer, Youngquist said that he had received $66,000 in
donations,[15] besides $2,600 received for reindeer sold in Alaska.
Youngquist also testified, as a member of the Good Hope

[13] MS. Record, pp. 871-899.

[14] *Abstract of Record,* pp. 307 f.

[15] This sum included $25,000 for North Park College buildings, $5000 as a
fund for needy students, $25,000 toward a hospital building, and $11,000 in
straight contributions. Besides these donations, Anderson gave $25,000 to
Walden College, a Swedish school in McPherson, Kansas, controlled by The
School Association of the Swedish Mission Conference of Kansas. For de-
tails, see *Kansas Missions-Tidning,* January, 1904, pp. 2-6, and *McPherson
Daily Republican,* December 23, 1904, p. 1. These files are in the Kansas State
Historical Society at Topeka.

Mining Company, that he had received payment for the shipment of supplies to Alaska.[16]

The most significant part of Youngquist's testimony pertained to his conversation with Brynteson and Lindblom. Youngquist said that when he had solicited funds from Brynteson, he had received the following reply: "Well, you must go for Mr. Anderson. He has got some more—he has got some gold there that belongs to the Mission, and when he has done right and turned over to you what doesn't belong to him, why, then I will see what I can do and will do for the Mission." Youngquist also related a conversation which he and Petterson had with Lindblom. After being asked for additional contributions, Lindblom retorted. "Why don't you people go after Mr. Anderson? He has got your claim; he has got your money. You get after him and then I will see what I will do afterwards. I will not promise you any more. Mr. Anderson has got plenty of your money and make him give you some."[17]

The most interesting witness was Constantine Uparazuck, the Eskimo boy for whom one claim had been originally intended. In preparation for the arbitration hearings, Hultberg had brought him down from Alaska in the fall of 1903. After five months in the states, he was homesick for his native village, his reindeer, and his simple life.

Constantine should have been a key witness for Hultberg's side. Unfortunately, his disabilities rendered his testimony untrustworthy. He was unable to give his age, could not remember when his brother died, and repeatedly answered that he didn't know or didn't remember. He admitted that he spoke through an interpreter up to 1900, but after his brother Gabriel died in that year he learned some English. Frequently he misunderstood questions, gave wrong answers, and asked for restatements of queries. Some idea of his testimony may be gained from the following responses:

> I didn't understand much this time good English. I am Eskimo. Eskimos never count how old they are. I don't

---

[16] The Good Hope Mining Company had sent John Hagelin as its representative to prospect for gold. Evidently, Hagelin did not utilize the goods when they arrived at Golovnin Bay, because Anderson paid for them.

[17] *Abstract of Record,* pp. 263, 266, 267.

remember how long time I first knew the Mission at Golovnin Bay. I don't know how big I was. I went to herd reindeer at the reindeer station. I don't know my father; somebody been killing him. Sometimes I was in school about an hour. I went to school in Golovnin Bay about three months. I been working with Hultberg. I don't been much to Golovnin Bay. Sometimes I be staying two nights and sometimes several nights, several days.

I can't think of it, how many months they are in a year. I don't remember what month it was that Hultberg talked to me about coming here. I forget what place we did go, from the office. I don't remember how long we stayed. Mr. Hultberg came to see me at Nome, I don't know how many times. Judge Soderberg sometimes came in the evening at the house in Nome. He talked to me sometimes. He told me a few words. Mr. Hultberg he sometimes told me a little about P. H. Anderson at Nome, a few words, and about No. 9. He talked about the Mission more than once. Walter Soderberg sometimes spoke to me a few words about P. H. Anderson and the Mission at Nome; not many times. I don't remember how many times. Albert Bjork spoke to me last fall at Nome about P. H. Anderson and the Mission and No. 9. And Hultberg's brother talked to me about the Mission and P. H. Anderson and No. 9 at Nome.[18]

It was evident from Constantine's replies that his memory was poor, his language deficient, and his understanding confused. What was more important, as brought out in the cross-examination, was that Constantine had been coached, that ideas had been put into his mind by Hultberg, Elliott, and even by Soderberg the lawyer, who was conducting the direct examination. It was difficult for the arbitrators, therefore, to ascertain what testimony was personal knowledge and what was hearsay.

Probably the most important statements made by Constantine pertained to No. 9 and its ownership. At one time he said:

Price had staked that No. 9 and turned [it over] to P. H. Anderson, to the Mission and the Eskimo boys, Gabriel

18 *Ibid.,* pp. 284, 290, 291-293, 297.

and I. He was telling me about he bought it to us, to the Mission and Gabriel and I. We can have No. 9 and Mission and Gabriel and I. I didn't understand much this time good English. He said he intend to give to the Mission and Gabriel and I all we want.[19]

Constantine spoke of the lawsuit on his own behalf in 1902. He said:

> I had talks with Hendrickson about No. 9 at that time. He told me about P. H. Anderson trying to keep that money. He said it belonged to Eskimo boys and to the Mission. I been signing papers. I don't know what kind of papers. He explained to me something. I don't understand. I might understand some words. Thuland was my lawyer. . . . I got $500, and I got a boat; too small. Sailing schooner. It takes three boys and myself to manage the boat. They said I got $500 a year for twenty-five year.[20]

Adolph V. Julin, a director of the Home of Mercy, spoke of several discussions he had with Dr. Johnson. Julin testified: "Dr. Johnson said we were foolish to think we could hold the claim in Alaska; if there is anybody there that should be entitled to it, it should be the Eskimo boys. That was in my office in 1901. I told him that we claimed it was ours."

Julin said that No. 9 was staked in Anderson's name for the Mission. "This is the way I heard it, and I always held onto that."[21]

S. A. Matson, a trustee of the Covenant since 1897, testified that he had attended meetings of the executive committee. He said that Anderson's position had been that he was not answerable to the committee or the denomination for No. 9. Matson spoke further about two meetings in the fall of 1902 when Anderson was confronted with letters of accusation regarding his moral conduct. According to Matson, Anderson had said that he had prayed to God to reveal to him whether No. 9 be-

19 *Ibid.*, pp. 286 f.
20 *Ibid.*, pp. 297 f.
21 MS. Record, pp. 1396-1402.

longed to him personally or to the Covenant, but at a subsequent meeting he had denied that he had prayed about the matter.[22]

John H. Humphrey, a dentist by profession, was in Nome in August, 1899. When he asked Anderson for a lease of part of No. 9, Anderson replied that he couldn't grant his request, since he lacked the authority to grant a lease on property which belonged to the Mission. Humphrey testified further that the mine was known as the Mission Claim and that he knew it belonged to the denomination.[23]

Albert Burke [Bjork], son of president C. A. Bjork, said that in December, 1899, he had walked with Anderson from Bowmanville to North Park College. In their discussion of mining, Burke asked how the business of No. 9 was getting along. According to Burke's testimony, Anderson replied:

> Of course, I do not intend to deny their right to the claim, but I think they might just as well let me have it and work it for them. I would be willing to turn over $50,000 this fall and turn over afterwards according to what the claim yields. I don't know whether it will be worked on a paying proposition—whether it will pay in the future or not, so I could not make any definite promise.[24]

Nels O. Hulberg's testimony was not too incriminating against Anderson, but it was the most interesting, judged by its historical content and by its revelation of the narrator himself.

Under the guidance of his own lawyer, Hultberg told of his arrival at Golovnin Bay on June 30, 1893; of his building a house at Cheenik and fixing up two rooms—one for a bedroom and the other for a combination living-room and schoolroom. He told of his search for gold in 1894 and 1895, in company with George Johanson. The big event of 1896 was the arrival of the government's reindeer, guided to Cheenik from Port Clarence by Hultberg and George T. Howard. In the summer

22 *Abstract of Record,* pp. 260-262.

23 *Ibid.,* pp. 310 f. Humphrey was a resident of Alameda, California.

24 Burke probably changed his name from Bjork. He had worked in Alaska for at least one summer. See *ibid.,* pp. 480 f.

of 1897 Anderson arrived as a teacher, and in the fall four men from San Francisco came to search for gold.[25]

Hultberg told of his trips in 1898 to search for gold. He recounted his two visits to Nome in January and August, 1898, his grub-staking Lindblom, and his decision to leave Alaska because of illness. He claimed credit for the first discovery of gold at Nome, said he knew the value of the district, and urged Brynteson, Lindblom, Anderson, and Kittilsen to return there. Hultberg had a written grub-stake contract with Lindblom for work on his mines on Melsing and Ophir Creeks in the Council City area (Discovery and Eldorado District), but he had no such written contract for Nome.[26]

That Hultberg urged others to go where he had prospected is certain, but that he deserved credit for what others discovered is less certain. Brynteson had been to Nome before, and had made up his own mind to return. Anderson and Kittilsen, joking with Hultberg about his imaginary discoveries and visionary schemes, decided not to go to Nome and thus missed out on an opportunity in September of becoming pioneer discoverers. Lindeberg decided to accompany Brynteson, as did Lindblom, whom Hultberg previously had grub-staked. According to Hultberg there was an oral agreement whereby Anderson would supply Brynteson and Lindblom with supplies which Hultberg owned personally. The failure of Anderson to do this, Hultberg asserted, cost him $300,000.[27] Hultberg testi-

---

[25] The four men were H. L. Blake, D. B. Libby, L. F. Melsing, and A. P. Mordaunt. See Leland H. Carlson, "The Discovery of Gold at Nome, Alaska," *The Pacific Historical Review,* September, 1946, p. 261.

[26] Hultberg sued Lindblom in a San Francisco court in 1899. Nothing seemed to have come from the suit except protests from Hultberg's acquaintances.

[27] On this issue Hultberg had brought suit on January 21, 1904, in the Circuit Court of Cook County, against Anderson for damages of $500,000. See N. O. Hultberg v. P. H. Anderson, General No. 247,848. These records are in the vault of the County Building in Chicago. Since this suit was instituted before the arbitration commission met, it was pending when the decision of April 13, 1904, was made. On the basis of the award of April 13, Hultberg filed a separate suit on April 15—General No. 250,666. In a third suit filed on April 16 by the White Star Mining Company, General No. 236,166, in the Superior Court of Cook County, the issues were similar, and by agreement of parties the two latter causes were tried as one in the Circuit Court (General No. 251,594). Anderson, too, had instituted a separate suit on February 18, 1904, because of Mellander's article against him (Minutes of Executive Committee and Sub-Committee, 1905-1910, October 18, 1907).

fied further that he left Golovnin Bay for a vacation in the States and Sweden, on August 31, 1898, just three weeks before the great strike on Anvil Creek. When he returned to Nome in 1899, he sought to pin Anderson down about what was to be done with No. 9. Hultberg related a conversation which occurred while he and Anderson were tramping across the tundra. Pressed about his plans for No. 9, Anderson said he intended to begin mining operations, and that he intended to pay himself $20 a day for his services as superintendent. Hultberg said that he contended that $15 was enough for a man who hitherto had earned only $2 a day. On another occasion, said Hultberg, he suggested that Anderson give Elliott a lease on No. 9, since Elliott was a missionary and since No. 9 was the Mission Claim.

The testimony of Hultberg indicated that personal differences existed which flared into animosity. There seems to have been a general incompatibility of interests and temperaments among the two men. Anderson considered himself to be an educated man but regarded Hultberg as ignorant and unlearned. When the two men staked claims in April, 1898, Hultberg claimed that he promised to give two-thirds of the proceeds to the Covenant, but Anderson "would not promise anything of that kind." On a grub-stake contract with Lindblom, Hultberg included Anderson's mines without consulting Anderson. When the two men disagreed on a policy, Hultberg said, "Anderson didn't say much about it. He was kind of growling about it and thought I was mixing up too much with other people." In 1899, according to Hultberg, "Anderson was very cross against me and treated me very inconsiderate." He even challenged Hultberg's right to resume his control of the Mission station. Again in 1900 there was almost open violence when Hultberg was told to mind his own business.[28]

Evidence on Behalf of Anderson

When P. H. Anderson appeared before the committee on March 7-8, the arbitrators had been listening for two weeks to evidence presented against him. It was interesting, therefore,

[28] MS. Record, pp. 1432-1496; 1514-1590. See p. 1547 especially for the verbal polemic.

for all concerned to see and hear the man around whom the controversy raged. Under questioning, Anderson told of his early life in Iowa and Kansas, his schooling at Des Moines, Enterprise, and Salina. He told of his conversion, his studies at North Park Academy from 1894 to 1896, and his work with Dr. Johnson at the Home of Mercy during the school year 1896-1897. On June 9, 1897, he said, he sailed for Alaska and arrived at Golovnin Bay on August 12.

Then Anderson recounted some of his Alaskan experiences. He told of his staking claims with Hultberg in the Council City area. It was on July 4, 1898, he said, that he first met Brynteson and Hagelin at St. Michael, and it was during August that he met Lindeberg and Lindblom. About a month later, on September 25, he met G. W. Price at St. Michael, informed him of the prospecting at Council City, and brought him to Cheenik in his own boat.

When Price left for Nome, Anderson asked him to stake a claim somewhere in the vicinity of where he staked for himself. Knowing that Price was an experienced miner, and considering him to be under obligation because of information given and free transportation, Anderson felt free to make the request. When Price returned on November 15, he said he had staked No. 8 for himself and No. 9 for his brother, R. L. Price, by a power of attorney. This latter claim he sold to Anderson for $20, and signed the necessary papers on November 17.[29]

Under cross-examination, the lawyers sought to show that Anderson was a trustee. They asked him why he should have two claims on Anvil Creek. To this question Anderson replied that he didn't know ahead of time where Price would stake a claim for him. Furthermore, he said, he wanted to help the Eskimo boys. During the examination a leading question was put to Anderson, when he was asked if Price had taken a claim in which the Eskimo boys could have an interest. To this question Anderson replied, "Yes," but his own lawyer, Judge Chytraus, took quick exception by adding "out of which you expected to do something for the Eskimo boys." Asked what

[29] MS. Record, pp. 504-511; 523 f.; 1601-1608; 1641-1645; 1844-1889; 1999-2071; 2114-2128. Anderson had a day book to consult for precise dates and events.

he had done for the Eskimo boys, Anderson said he had given them small amounts of money from time to time, a sailing boat, and a small "knock-down house." He added the point that because the boys had been seen in gambling and drinking resorts at Nome, he considered it undesirable to give them too much money.[30]

Then Anderson was asked about points brought out in previous evidence. He denied that he had ever made statements to the effect that he held No. 9 as a trustee. He took exception to the assertions of Hultberg and Karlson about the conversation on the tundra and about paying himself $20 a day. He disavowed any assertion of praying for light regarding the ownership of No. 9, and he took issue with the statement of Albert Burke [Bjork] that in conversation with the latter he had admitted Covenant ownership.

Questioned about his financial affairs, Anderson said that No. 2 Above had yielded about $75,000 and that No. 9 had netted about $335,000. He told of $50,000 invested in the South American Diamond Company, of $10,000 in the State Bank of Chicago, and of $12,500 invested in a Kansas farm. It was brought out that he had donated about $95,000 to Covenant enterprises, and had made loans to others for at least $7,800.[31]

It was natural that Dr. C. W. Johnson should testify on behalf of Anderson. Dr. Johnson had been connected with the Home of Mercy since its beginning in 1886. In 1896-1897 he had worked closely with Anderson and had taught him the rudiments of medical practice in preparation for his work in Alaska.

Dr. Johnson told of his hopes of obtaining enough money to build a hospital in the Lake View district of Chicago. He spoke of $25,000 received from Anderson and $25,000 received from Brynteson. In 1902, he testified, he became general manager of No. 9 and on January 3, 1903, he purchased all the stock in Anderson's firm—the White Star Mining Company of California—on a "bed rock" contract, whereby An-

---

[30] *Ibid.,* pp. 2041, 2061.
[31] Compare testimony of C. A. Youngquist.

derson would be paid $100,000 out of income from the claims as they were developed. He denied the existence of any secret understanding and said there was no agreement for transferring back the stock.[32]

For several reasons the testimony of David Nyvall was especially interesting. Of all the Covenant officials, Nyvall was the only one who testified on behalf of Anderson. As secretary of the Covenant, Nyvall had written the letters for the executive committee and had carried on the correspondence with such men as Anderson, Hultberg, and Karlson. With Bjork, he had signed the release given to Anderson. As one who possessed detailed knowledge, as one who who had visited the Alaskan field in 1903, and as one who had strongly opposed the initiation of a lawsuit, Nyvall was indeed a key man.

Under questioning, Nyvall conceded that "it was an exceedingly unpopular thing to be known as the advocate and champion of P. H. Anderson." The examiner asked Nyvall if it was not true that, as the strongest and most prominent man in the Covenant, he had lost his position of leadership because of his stand on the gold case. Nyvall disagreed with this conclusion, cited the pressures exerted in 1903 to have him continue as secretary, and then added: "I do not see any point at all there in it, whether I am popular or not. The question with me is whether I have a good conscience or not."[33]

Nyvall was accused of showing more favoritism to Anderson than to Hultberg. To this charge, Nyvall replied that he counted both men as friends and that his attitudes about both of them had varied. On some issues he agreed, on others he disagreed, but in the main his feelings were kindly, he said, toward both men.

What must have been a bombshell at the hearings was a question from Hultberg's lawyer, Soderberg, who asked Nyvall if he ever had stated that the service which he had rendered to Anderson amounted to obstructing justice. When Nyvall challenged such a statement, Soderberg produced a letter written by Nyvall to his father on February 2, 1903. In this letter

[32] *Abstract of Record,* pp. 362, 474-479.
[33] MS. Record, pp. 1945 f.

Nyvall had discussed freely the issues of No. 9 and had concluded that Anderson was in the wrong. He had written about
Anderson as follows:

> He has himself acknowledged the debt he stands in to
> the Eskimo boys by settling with them, as it is called. It
> was Dr. C. W. Johnson, formerly physician at the Home
> [of Mercy], who last summer did him that service when
> he was sued by the Eskimo boys, namely: to settle with
> them for a sum of about $25,000 besides the large sums
> which the attorneys for both parties of course demanded,
> in order to permit a settlement. It is possible, however,
> that this settlement, as before the law, put an end to this
> question and that it cannot be further taken up. At all
> events, I have no desire to concern myself any further,
> but I leave him to his own conscience as the worst judge
> he can encounter.[34]

The implication of this letter was that Anderson seemed to
have bought off the Eskimo boys, and that despite a bad conscience he continued to hold No. 9 Above. Nyvall seemed,
therefore, to be in a position where he sided in with a man
who was in the wrong. Asked about this, Nyvall clarified his
entire position by making the following statement:

> I simply was not certain as to the ownership of that
> mine, and that was what decided my siding or not siding.
> I never championed Mr. Anderson's cause in it, but I was
> always uncertain in my mind whether we had a right to
> the property or not. And then I reasoned this way, that it
> was wiser for us not to push the question as a legal claim
> at all, but to handle it in a brotherly and friendly way.

[34] This letter represented Nyvall's views in February, 1903. Nyvall had
vacillated in his mind about the issues of No. 9, but the confessions of Anderson in November, 1902, and the news of the termination of the Eskimo
suit arriving that same fall, had precipitated an opinion which Nyvall sent
to his father. Nyvall said that this letter represented opinion, not fact, and
had no public significance. Mellander's action, however, of copying this letter
from Nyvall's copybook without consulting Nyvall was an unfair procedure
for which he was asked to apologize.

So far as Nyvall was concerned, the letter simply indicated his view that
Anderson by no means was blameless. The fact that Nyvall was unwilling to
testify against Anderson, despite his personal feelings, proves that Nyvall
distinguished between principle and personality.

This has been my standpoint from the beginning to the end, and this is my standpoint today.[35]

Nyvall went on to say that he never saw any wisdom in becoming involved in a lawsuit. He said he did not pass judgment on the case because that depended on the facts, which he did not have. When the lawyer asked him if it would be wise to recover $300,000 taken from the Covenant, Nyvall replied: "It might be wise to get in peace $100,000 better [rather?] than fight for $300,000 and get nothing." When the lawyer countered by asking—"if it is possible to bring a man to justice who has taken $200,000 from the Mission, that would be just?" —Nyvall parried: "You beg the question there."[36]

It was unfortunate that John Brynteson did not testify before the arbitrators. He was the only man who had been on all three prospecting trips. His statements, as quoted by Petterson and Youngquist, had resulted in the assertion of Covenant ownership of No. 9. Had he been present, undoubtedly he could have cleared up some disputed points. A telegram was sent to him, but he was apprehensive, sent a letter in reply, and did not appear before the arbitrators.[37]

There was some independent testimony from Brynteson, nevertheless, which was utilized. In October, 1900, Brynteson had given a deposition before Judge C. S. Johnson and W. T. Hume. The reason for the deposition was that Anderson's mine, No. 2 Above, had been jumped by O. José Comptois. To defend Anderson's claims, Brynteson testified in Nome, and his deposition—amounting to ninety-seven typed pages—was introduced in 1904 on behalf of Anderson. This deposition carried weight, since it had been given before any dispute had arisen with Hultberg. Its independent value, therefore, was unassailable.

Brynteson told of his arrival in the United States in 1887, his work in Michigan and Wisconsin, and his decision to go to

---

[35] MS. Record, p. 1962.

[36] *Ibid.*, p. 1940. That is, Soderberg was assuming that Anderson had stolen the claim. Nyvall in his reply indicated that Soderberg was assuming as a conclusion what was only a premise.

[37] *Abstract of Record*, p. 367. Judge Chytraus said: "You can get Brynteson here if you will guarantee him against any suit."

Alaska. In company with John Hagelin, who represented the Good Hope Mining Company, he arrived at St. Michael on July 3, 1898, and at Golovnin Bay about July 22. He then related the story of his three trips to Nome, the prospecting on the first trip in August, the staking in September, and the re-staking in October.

One interesting part of his testimony was his assertion that in September No. 6 Above was the uppermost claim staked on the creek. In other words, No. 7, No. 8, and No. 9 were not staked in September and restaked in October. Rather, they were staked for the first time in October by Kittilsen and Price. This testimony would imply that it may have been intended to stake for the Eskimo boys on the September trip, but that no actual staking took place. Legally, this is true, and according to Brynteson it was also actually true, despite the intention in the minds of the prospectors.[38]

Another interesting part of Brynteson's testimony related to the matter of provisions. Hultberg's claim had been that it was his discoveries and his supplies which made possible the great strike on Anvil Creek. But Brynteson denied any grub-staking arrangement. He said that he had purchased his own provisions and at all times was independent. Lindeberg had his own supplies, and Dr. Kittilsen had purchased goods from the schooner *Moonlight*. Some additional provisions had been purchased from Anderson and from John Dexter's trading post. So far as Lindblom was concerned, Brynteson said that Lindblom used the supplies belonging to the party.[39]

The net effect of Brynteson's deposition of October, 1900, and of his equivocal testimony before the Covenant committee in February of the same year, was that he regarded Anderson as the owner of No. 9 and that he thought that the Eskimo boys and the denomination should share in the proceeds. Just what

[38] It is conceivable that Brynteson knew of a September staking of Nos. 7, 8, and 9, but that he deliberately forgot this fact in the belief that staking for the Eskimos was illegal. My own belief is that the plan of staking for the boys was approved in principle but not carried out in September. Dr. Kittilsen, who owned No. 7, and who had nothing to lose by speaking truthfully, said that he found no stakes above No. 6.

[39] MS. Record, pp. 2217-2314.

proportion each should have was a question no one could answer objectively.

Judge Charles S. Johnson, attorney for the White Star Mining Company of California and for Anderson in the suit brought by the Eskimos in 1902, testified before the arbitrators. He spoke of his long association with Alaska and his knowledge of mining law. Asked about the right of natives to hold claims, he said:

> I found the rule to be that if the natives had located or taken a claim in their own names, they could not be disturbed in the possession by any one but the United States, but I also found that a court of equity would not lend its aid to erect a trust in real estate in favor of one who could not ultimately acquire title to the land. If they got possession they could defend their possessions against everybody except the United States, and a trust created for their benefit would not be good.

Judge Johnson said further that he had represented nearly every claim on Anvil Creek. Whenever a claim was rich, there was a fight about it. "That was the first evidence of its value." He spoke further about the laws regulating Alaskan mining, especially the code enacted June 6, 1900, and he described in detail the requirements for a valid staking. A mining claim, he said, was real property according to the decisions of the courts.[40]

A. N. Kittilsen was a member of the party that made the famous strike in October, 1898. A medical doctor by training, he had come to Alaska in 1896 as a government employee, to care for the health of the Laps and Eskimos, and to serve as assistant superintendent of the reindeer station at Port Clarence and later near Unalakleet.

The most pertinent statements of Dr. Kittilsen related to his prospecting. He said that when Hultberg returned from Nome in August he was enthusiastic about the prospects. Hultberg encouraged Kittilsen to go up to Nome, but the latter was dubious, as indicated in his statement to the arbitrators:

[40] *Abstract of Record,* p. 337.

I never took very much stock in his report for the different districts, because he always found great prospects wherever he went, reported good prospects when he came back. He never brought any gold back with him that I saw.[41]

The reports of Brynteson, Lindeberg, and Lindblom, however, were more than enough to convince Kittilsen, and on October 12 he set out for Nome with these men, together with Tornensis, Price, and Constantine. Kittilsen testified that he had a large amount of provisions which he had recently purchased.[42] Of these he sold some to Brynteson and Lindblom, and received payment from Price for meals eaten. When the party arrived at Nome, Kittilsen was elected recorder of the Cape Nome Mining District. Asked about No. 7, which he staked for himself, and about No. 8 and 9, Kittilsen said he had heard that Lindeberg had staked No. 7 for him in September and that someone had staked No. 8 and No. 9 for the Eskimo boys. But, he added, there were no stakes beyond the upper end of No. 6. When the old stakes were pulled up, there were none to pull up on Nos. 7, 8, and 9. So far as the Covenant or the Mission was concerned, Kittilsen testified, he never knew anything about such a claim until 1900.

The key witness for Anderson was G. W. Price. He told of his prospecting in the Kotzebue Sound region, of his meeting Anderson at St. Michael on September 25, 1898, of his boat trip to Golovnin Bay with Anderson, and of his week's visit to the Council City area. He then related the story of his invitation to go to Nome. Dr. Kittilsen and Anderson were instrumental in arranging his departure on October 12. Since the boat was already loaded with supplies, Price paid cash for his meals. On their arrival at Nome, he noted that the claims were improperly staked and included too much territory. All agreed on restaking. According to Price, there were no stakes above No. 6.

When Price was asked what the reason was for letting him

41 *Ibid.,* pp. 403 f.

42 He bought a two years' supply from Franklin and Griffith, two men on the schooner *Moonlight.*

in on the newly discovered claims, he replied that his knowledge of mining and his agreement to stake No. 9 for Anderson were the considerations. When he was asked why Anderson should have two claims on the same creek, he replied: "The only reason that anyone gave that Anderson should have two claims was that he said he wanted something for the Eskimo boys, Constantine and Gabriel, and wanted another claim, and that seemed to be satisfactory to all others." Asked about the right of Eskimo boys to hold claims, Price said he had given it as his opinion that an Eskimo couldn't hold a claim. He said further that he had never in his life heard that a claim had been staked for them or either of them. As to the denomination, he said that any possible interest that the Mission might have was never mentioned, and as to Hultberg there "was absolutely no talk at all about a grub stake." About Anderson's ownership he said:

> I located it for my brother and sold it to P. H. Anderson afterwards. The intention, before I staked it in my brother's name, was that it should be for P. H. Anderson. I was to sell it to P. H. Anderson. The price was not agreed upon until afterwards.[43]

On the value of No. 8 and No. 9, Price testified that originally he considered No. 8 worth about $15,000 and No. 9 about $4,000. In view of the greatly increased value of No. 9, Judge Soderberg asked Price if he had ever considered what a serious matter it would be if Anderson lost the case. Price replied: "I consider it a case of blackmail from start to finish, and don't have any idea that he will lose it."[44]

The Arbitration Award

On March 18 both sides completed their presentation of witnesses and terminated their rebuttal arguments. Adjournment was made until March 26, when arguments of the lawyers were begun. By April 7 the arguments were concluded, and on

43 *Ibid.,* p. 392.
44 *Ibid.,* p. 389.

April 13 the arbitrators met to discuss their conclusions. Mr. Lane, who was not a lawyer, did not prepare an opinion, but Gilbert and Pence drew up their conclusions in writing. The two lawyers discussed questions of fact and of law. They both professed willingness [in theory] to change their opinions if they found themselves in the wrong, but [in fact] they were unable to agree on the conclusions to be drawn from the evidence, or on the application of equitable and legal principles to the facts obtained. The result was a divided opinion. On April 13 the arbitrators announced their decision, Gilbert and Lane voting for Hultberg and Pence for Anderson. The terms of the award were as follows:

First. With respect to the claims and demands of said Nels O. Hultberg, so far as the White Star Mining Company, of Illinois, and Claes W. Johnson are concerned, we decide that said Nels O. Hultberg is the owner of that certain placer mine and mining claim, mentioned in said agreement, known as and called "No. 9 Above on Anvil Creek," situate in the Cape Nome Mining and Recording District in the District of Alaska, and we award to him, said Nels O. Hultberg, the said placer mine and mining claim, and direct the said White Star Mining Company, of Illinois, to forthwith convey and deliver possession thereof to the said Nels O. Hultberg, and we further decide that the output of said placer mine and mining claim and the gold extracted therefrom during the mining season of 1903, after deducting therefrom a sufficient amount of gold or moneys to pay and defray all the expenses of the said White Star Mining Company, of Illinois, and said Claes W. Johnson in operating said mine and mining claim, including labor, and material purchased therefor during said time, and also after deducting therefrom the further sum of $9,000.00, which said last mentioned sum is to be had and received by said Johnson out of said output for his personal services, which said output, after making the deductions aforesaid, is the sum of Twenty-six Thousand Dollars ($26,000.00), belongs to said Nels O. Hultberg and we award said sum to him, the same to be accounted for by said White Star Mining Company, of

Illinois, and by said Claes W. Johnson and turned over by them to said Nels O. Hultberg immediately.

Second. With respect to the claims of said Nels O. Hultberg against Peter H. Anderson, we decide that said Nels O. Hultberg is entitled to recover from said Peter H. Anderson the sum of Two Hundred Thirty-two Thousand Two Hundred Dollars ($232,200.00) and we award said sum to said Nels O. Hultberg to be paid to him immediately by said Peter H. Anderson.

Third. We award to the said Nels O. Hultberg the sum of Two Hundred Fifty Dollars ($250.00) to be paid by said White Star Mining Company, of Illinois, and Claes W. Johnson jointly, and the further sum of Two Hundred Fifty Dollars ($250.00) to be paid by said Peter H. Anderson as his statutory costs and expenditures incurred by him in and about said arbitration, the said sums amounting in all to Five Hundred Dollars ($500.00), being agreed upon as correct and just by the said parties, and all other costs and expenses of said arbitration having by the agreement of the parties been paid out of moneys furnished said arbitrators for that purpose by said White Star Mining Company, of Illinois, Claes W. Johnson and Peter H. Anderson, the amount so paid and furnished by said White Star Mining Company, of Illinois, and said Johnson being Fourteen Hundred Thirty-six Dollars and Twenty-five Cents ($1,436.25), and the amount so paid by said Peter H. Anderson being Three Thousand Seven Hundred Fifty Dollars ($3,750.00).

We make the foregoing award as a full and complete decision and determination of all the matters of difference between the said parties submitted to us by said agreement of special submission to arbitration.

WITNESS our hands and seals this 13th day of April, A. D. 1904.

    (Signed)   Hiram T. Gilbert.   (Seal.)
    (Signed)   David F. Lane.   (Seal.)[45]

[45] The award is printed in The Supreme Court of the United States, October Term 1906, No. 647, Claes W. Johnson v. N. O. Hultberg *et al.*,

The Opinions of the Arbitrators

Gilbert held that No. 8 and No. 9 were staked in September, and that the purpose was not to enrich the Eskimo boys but to benefit the Covenant. He concluded that Price located No. 9 for Anderson, who was to hold it in trust for the Covenant. Particular stress was given to oral statements made by Anderson in 1899 that No. 9 belonged to the Covenant. These statements, Gilbert argued, were indicative of Anderson's attitude until the manifest riches of No. 9 were known.

In the matter of the release of 1901, Gilbert contended that it was invalid, partly because of false misrepresentations and partly because of neglect on the part of those executing the release. Anderson was a trustee for the Covenant, and the resulting trust that followed his acquisition of title to No. 9 precluded his right to secure a release for himself. Consequently, No. 9 and its income to date should be given to Hultberg as the assignee of the Covenant.[46]

Transcript of Record, pp. 90-93. The figures illustrating the award are as follows:

Dr. C. W. Johnson's receipts from No. 9 in 1903		$77,500.00
Paid to Anderson	$25,000.00	
Paid to lawyers to settle fees on Eskimo suit	17,500.00	
Allowed for personal expenses and salary for Dr. Johnson	9,000.00	
Total allowances		51,500.00
Balance due Hultberg from Dr. Johnson		$26,000.00
Income of P. H. Anderson from No. 9 Above		$335,000.00
(1899—$40,000; 1900—$175,000; 1901—$40,000; 1902—$80,000)		
Received from Dr. Johnson in 1903		25,000.00
Cost of settling judgment in 1903		17,500.00
Total receipts		$377,500.00
Donations to Covenant enterprises	$95,000.00	
Lawyers' fees in 1902	13,000.00	
Cost of settling judgment in 1903	17,500.00	
Payment to Eskimos	2,500.00	
Annuity set aside for Eskimos	12,000.00	
Bench claim and miscellaneous costs	5,300.00	145,300.00
Balance due Hultberg from P. H. Anderson		$232,200.00

The cost of arbitration is seen in the following figures:

Amount deposited by Dr. Johnson, Anderson, and Hultberg ($4,000 each)		$12,000.00
Cost for arbitrators, stenographer, travel	$5,186.25	
Credit allowed to the winner (original deposit)	4,000.00	
General costs agreed upon; to be given to the winner	500.00	
Total expenses and credits		9,686.25
To be applied to judgment against Dr. Johnson		$ 2,313.75

[46] Gilbert's opinion is printed in The Supreme Court of Illinois, October Term 1904, No. 3912, White Star Mining Company v. N. O. Hultberg *et al.*, *Statement of the Case. Opinion of Judge Frederick A. Smith. Opinion of*

The opinion of arbitrator Pence differed sharply from that of Gilbert. Pence argued that the Eskimo boys never acquired any interest in No. 8 and No. 9. In proof of this, he contended that Brynteson, Kittilsen, and Price—all primary witnesses— asserted that on the September trip the uppermost claim to be staked was No. 6. Furthermore, said Pence, the notices of claims were all filed for record in the office of the district recorder, and these reveal that Nos. 1-6 were located on September 22 and Nos. 7-9 on October 18. If the Eskimo boys, there- fore, never acquired any interest, the Covenant could have no interest either as beneficiary.[47]

Pence minimized the value of the statements made by Karl- son, Elliott, Humphrey, Constantine, and Hultberg. Though all these men were in Alaska, not one of them was present at the September or October stakings. They relied on what they heard from others, and their hearsay testimony varied. Some argued that No. 9 belonged to the Eskimo boys, some to the boys in trust for the Alaska Mission or for the denomination, some to the Covenant, some to the Alaska Mission, some to both, and some to all three.

On the matter of Anderson's admissions, Pence argued that his statements about doing something to help the Eskimo boys could easily be changed into doing something on behalf of the boys as owners of No. 9. He contended that oral statements in the eyes of the law did not have the value of written deeds.[48]

So far as provisions were concerned, Pence said that Kittil- sen and Lindeberg had their own supplies, and that the trader Dexter had sold additional items to the men. Admittedly, some of the supplies came from the Mission station, but since these were kept together, and since Anderson owned $700 worth as his annual salary, it could be argued that none of the supplies were donated by the station. Even the use of the Mission

---

Arbitrator Hiram T. Gilbert, pp. 52-92. The opinions of Lane and Pence simply cancelled out each other. Pence, of course, disagreed with Gilbert's conclusion. Since Pence's opinions were similar to those of Justice W. H. Sanborn, who awarded the decision to Anderson in 1919, I shall withhold the counter arguments until a later chapter, which will summarize the history of the litigation that developed from 1904 to 1919.

[47] See *Abstract of Record,* pp. 374 f; Appendix, pp. 60 f.

[48] *Ibid.,* Appendix, pp. 63-66, 69 f.

schooner was compensated for by the building of the school house by the miners.

Regarding the release and the Covenant's repudiation of it, Pence held strong convictions. He wrote:

> Although I believe the members of that [executive] committee to be honest in now asserting a claim against Mr. Anderson, yet as a body their action cannot be otherwise considered than as immoral [unethical?]. We do not think this committee fully comprehends the claim they are making. In any ordinary business affairs conducted by the ordinary man, such an action would be condemned by every court, and all courts, as highly immoral and unjust. They have led Mr. Anderson into a course of action which he expressly states in his letters he would not take except upon their assent to his proposition that the Covenant had no claim, and the executive committee accepted of the donation offered to them upon that basis, and received the money, and they are now forever estopped, not only in point of law and equity, but in point of good morals, from ever asserting any claim again touching this matter.[49]

Concluding that there was no express trust, since Anderson had given no written assignment, that there was no constructive trust, since the sending of Anderson as a missionary did not create any fiduciary relation between him and the denomination, and that there was no resulting trust, since the alleged beneficiary [the Covenant] paid no money before or at the time that the title was vested in Anderson, Pence held that Hultberg had no claim whatsoever on behalf of himself or his assignor, the Covenant.[50]

---

[49] *Ibid.,* Appendix, p. 80.
[50] *Ibid., Appendix,* pp. 67-78.

THE APPEAL TO THE COURTS

THE APPEAL TO THE COURTS

Thus far in our story of the Alaskan mine, we have related the discovery of gold at Nome, the staking and restaking of No. 9 Above, the account of the first mining season of 1899, the beginnings of the controversy, the developments in 1900, and the discussions culminating in the signing of the release in 1901. We have also presented the story of the Eskimo lawsuit of 1902, the decision of the Covenant to assign its claim of ownership to Hultberg, and the joining of issues in the arbitration commission's meetings in 1904. We have seen that the arbitration commission heard testimony on behalf of Hultberg and Anderson, and that on the basis of this evidence the decision was given in favor of Hultberg on April 13, 1904. By this verdict, Hultberg was awarded $232,200 from Anderson, and $26,000 from Dr. Johnson, as well as $500 in costs agreed upon by both parties.

Although the arbitration commission's findings were intended to end the issue in dispute, they were actually the beginning of legal battles that extended over sixteen years. It is the purpose of this chapter to trace the history of this protracted and bitterly-contested litigation.

Even before the meeting of the arbitration commission in 1904, Anderson had been involved in legal difficulties. As early as 1899 he had found it necessary to defend No. 2 Above and No. 9 Above against jumpers' claims presented to the U. S. commissioner's court. In 1900 he had been the victim of injustice when Judge Noyes appointed his friend McKenzie receiver of No. 2 Above. This issue was settled in Anderson's favor by 1901, but in the following year he was forced into court once more by the Eskimo lawsuit. Again he was victorious, but his troubles were not ended. Hultberg, determined to seek vengeance, was insistent on securing from the Covenant an assignment of No. 9 Above, and succeeded in bringing about the arbitration agreement of 1903.

Even before the arbitration commission began its hearings on February 20, 1904, Hultberg had requested a praecipe in an action of trespass, dated and filed January 21, 1904.[1] In the bill of complaint, Hultberg averred that he had made a stipulation with Anderson whereby the latter agreed to act as an agent for him in furnishing "certain tools, supplies, provisions, etc., left by the plaintiff [Hultberg] with the defendant [Anderson] at the place aforesaid [Cheenik], for the purpose of enabling the said Eric O. Lindblom and others to prospect for gold and other precious minerals and metals on Anvil Creek, Dry Creek, Glacier Creek, Snow Gulch, Rock Creek, Dexter Creek and other creeks."

Hultberg averred further that he had a contract with Lindblom by which he was to receive one-half of the proceeds from any mining claims located by such prospectors. Although Anderson knew it was his duty to supply Lindblom, yet he "did wrongfully and collusively and maliciously, with the intention of cheating and defrauding the said plaintiff out of his just rights in the premises, refuse and neglect to furnish such supplies, tools, provisions, etc., to the said Eric O. Lindblom. Therefore, claimed Hultberg, he was damaged to the extent of $500,000, for which amount he sues.[2]

Anderson's reply was filed on June 2, 1904. He denied

---

[1] The bill of complaint was not filed until May 10, 1904. This case is No. 247,848 in the vault of the Circuit Court of Cook County. See *Abstract of Record,* pp. 193, 499, 507. See also White Star Mining Company of Illinois vs. Nels O. Hultberg *et al. Brief and Argument for Appellant,* Supreme Court of Illinois, No. 3912, p. 135, and Manuscript Record, p. 2432.

[2] Hultberg and his attorney, Nels Soderberg, evidently were making wild charges. They were unable to produce any grubstake contract which would substantiate their allegations against Anderson. So far as Lindblom was concerned, Hultberg did have a grubstake contract, but this applied to the Council City area. So far as Nome and Anvil Creek were concerned, there was no contract made. Hultberg probably claimed that when he had left Cheenik on August 31, 1898, he had given oral instructions to Anderson. Parol evidence, however, if not confirmed by independent witnesses, is liable to much abuse and distortion, since a man could claim anything on his *ipse dixit.*

the allegations and asserted he was not guilty of any of the charges made.[3]

On February 18, 1904, Anderson initiated a suit against the Covenant and its executive committee. The reason for this action was an article published on March 2, 1903, by Axel Mellander in the denominational publication, *Missionären*. Since Mellander had leveled charges of moral delinquency against Anderson, the latter considered himself unjustly maligned, and asked $75,000 damages. The suit lingered on in the Circuit Court of Cook County until November 15, 1909, when it was finally dropped. The only tangible result was that the lawyers collected their fees, with Attorney Harris F. Williams obtaining at least $1000 from the Covenant for his services.[4]

It is apparent, therefore, that at least two suits were pending in the spring of 1904 when the arbitration commission was hearing testimony. When the commission made its award on April 13, 1904, the legal battle was just beginning. Just two days later, on April 15, Hultberg filed a copy of the award in the Circuit Court of Cook County, in order to obtain a judgment thereupon.[5] Specifically, Hultberg sought to obtain Anderson's apartment building on Wilson Avenue, his safety deposit box at the Chamber of Commerce Safety Vault Company, his two farms in Dickinson County, Kansas, his stock in the Brazilian Diamond, Gold and Developing Company, his fifty shares of the State Bank of Chicago, besides money on deposit there, and also a sum over $10,000 belonging to Frideborg A. Anderson [Mrs. P. H. Anderson], on deposit in Aktiebolaget—Göteborgs Bank in Sweden.

[3] On April 18, 1907, a stipulation was filed in the Circuit Court of Cook County. It was agreed that the case was to be passed, since other related litigation was pending, but with the proviso that the case could be taken up again by either party on five days' notice.

[4] Minutes of the Executive Committee and Sub-Committee, 1905-1910, meetings of October 18, 1907, and November 22, 1909. The pages are not numbered in this manuscript, which is in the Covenant archives. See also *Förbundets Tjugonde Årsmöte i Paxton, Illinois. Rapport till Församlingarna, 1904* (Minneapolis, 1904), p. 87. The records reveal two payments of $500 each to Attorney Williams. There may have been more.

[5] Nels O. Hultberg vs. White Star Mining Company, Claes W. Johnson, and Peter H. Anderson. This is case No. 250,666 in the Circuit Court of Cook County.

On April 16, the White Star Mining Company, Claes W. Johnson, and Peter H. Anderson entered their appearance in the Circuit Court of Cook County and moved the court to vacate, set aside, and annul the award.[6]

The Superior Court of Cook County

On April 16, 1904, just one day after Hultberg had begun his suit in the Circuit Court of Cook County, the White Star Mining Company presented its original bill of complaint in the Superior Court of Cook County.[7] In this bill the company asserted its ownership of No. 9 Above, and denied any rightful interest therein by either Hultberg or the Covenant. The bill contended that the award of the arbitrators was null and void because it embraced matters expressly excluded by the articles of submission of August 12, 1903, and by the rulings of the arbitrators themselves. Furthermore, the award was characterized by fraud, embodied errors both of fact and of law, and deprived the plaintiff of his rightful property. Therefore, the bill prayed for an injunction against the Merchants' Loan and Trust Company to restrain it from paying out money on deposit to Hultberg. The bill further alleged the intention of Hultberg to enforce the collection of the award. It prayed for a restraining order to prevent Hultberg from interfering with the possession and operation of No. 9 Above, and requested the court to set aside, vacate, and annul the pretended award.[8]

[6] Supreme Court of the United States, October Term, 1906, No. 647: Claes W. Johnson, plaintiff in error, vs. Nels O. Hultberg, Swedish Evangelical Mission Covenant of America, *et al., Transcript of Record,* pp. 38, 39, 156. See also Circuit Court of the United States, Northern District of Illinois, Eastern Division, Peter H. Anderson *et al.* vs. The Swedish Evangelical Mission Covenant of America, Nels O. Hultberg, and the Merchants' Loan and Trust Company, *Exhibits,* p. 21 and note 3.

[7] The Circuit Court and the Superior Court are both county courts and are of approximately coordinate jurisdiction. The White Star Mining Company may have been influenced in its selection of a court by the fact that its adviser was Axel Chytraus, who was a judge of the Superior Court, who owned ten shares of stock in the mining company, and who was the attorney for both Dr. Johnson and Anderson during the sessions of the arbitration commission.

[8] The original bill of complaint is in the records of the Superior Court. It is printed in the Supreme Court of the United States, No. 647, Claes W. Johnson vs. Nels O. Hultberg *et al., Transcript of Record,* pp. 78-101.

In response to the bill of the White Star Mining Company, the defendants filed their appearances within twenty days. Hultberg and the Covenant filed on May 3, the Merchants' Loan and Trust Company on May 4, Johnson and Anderson on May 5. On May 10, the lawyers for the defendant [Hultberg] notified the lawyers for the complainant [White Star Mining Company of Illinois] that they would petition Judge Theodore Brentano to remove the case from the calendar of the Superior Court. By agreement of the parties, an order was entered on May 11, in the Superior Court, whereby the case was transferred to the Circuit Court of Cook County.[9]

The Circuit Court of Cook County

The transference of the case was completed on May 16, when the first amended bill of complaint was filed in the Circuit Court of Cook County by the White Star Mining Company of Illinois.[10] On May 17 the answers of Hultberg and the Swedish Evangelical Mission Covenant of America to the first amended bill were filed, and on the same day their cross-bills were introduced.[11] Hearings began before Judge Frederick A. Smith on May 19 and continued until June 13. The main contentions or issues as presented to the court by Anderson and Johnson were as follows:

1. The arbitrators, Gilbert and Lane, decided the issues before them "upon irrelevant, incompetent, improper

---

[9] *Abstract of Record*, p. 1. The reason for the change of courts seems to have been the desire of consolidating the pending cases. Another plausible reason would be that of avoiding any charge of sympathy from the colleagues of Axel Chytraus.

[10] The order of Judge Brentano of the Superior Court was filed on May 16 in the Circuit Court and approved on May 17 by Judge Frederick A. Smith of the latter court.

[11] The Merchants' Loan and Trust Company filed its cross-bill on May 20. On May 23, Johnson, Anderson, and the White Star Mining Company filed their replications, and on the same date Anderson and Johnson filed answers to the cross-bills of Hultberg and the Covenant. On May 31, Johnson and Anderson filed cross-bills. The answers to these, in turn, were filed on June 2. Finally on June 13, the White Star Mining Company of Illinois filed its second amended bill.

The various pleadings are in the Manuscript Record, in the *Abstract of Record,* and in the *Transcript of Record*. The original papers are in the vaults in the Cook County Criminal Court building, Twenty-Sixth and California, Chicago, case No. 251,594.

111

and hearsay evidence, and in some particulars without any evidence whatever upon which to base their conclusions of fact."

2. The arbitrators were in error in their computations of costs and expenses, which were unjustly assigned to Anderson and Johnson.

3. There was collusion on the part of Gilbert, Lane and Hultberg to deprive Anderson and Johnson of a fair and full hearing with reference to an accounting of the costs of mining operations, a charge which makes the arbitration award fraudulent.

4. The Covenant is legally wrong in asserting that it was beyond the power of the president and the secretary, acting in conjunction with the executive board and the annual meeting of delegates, to execute a release in favor of Anderson.

5. The Covenant was further wrong in holding that as a nonprofit organization it was entitled to property acquired by its missionary or that such a missionary was a trustee accountable to the corporation for profits made.

6. Dr. Johnson was never authorized, directed or empowered by the directors of the White Star Mining Company of Illinois to sign and execute the articles of agreement for arbitration.

7. The evidence before the arbitrators clearly indicated that neither Hultberg nor the Covenant had any right, title, claim, or interest in No. 9 Above.

8. Whereas the articles of agreement for arbitration were signed on August 12, 1903, the Covenant did not assign its interest to Hultberg until September 8, 1903. Therefore Hultberg had no right or interest on August 12, 1903.

9. The assignment by the Covenant on September 8, 1903, repudiates and disregards its release, executed in favor of Anderson on August 16, 1901,

which fully released and discharged Anderson from any and all claims.

10. Hultberg's claims are similar to those advanced by the Eskimo boys. Since the Eskimo lawsuit was settled in favor of Anderson, it follows that the claims of Hultberg are groundless.

With these contentions Hultberg and the Covenant disagreed sharply. They asserted that the arbitrators had based their findings on competent evidence, that they had given full opportunity for a fair and honest accounting, that the Covenant was legally correct in repudiating the release because of false and inadequate information supplied by Anderson. They contended that Anderson's trustee relationship was proved by his own admissions to various individuals, and that the arbitrators had so found. They also asserted that Dr. Johnson acted with full knowledge and acquiescence of his company since Judge Chytraus had aided in drawing up the articles of submission and since Anderson had affixed his signature to them when Johnson had returned from Alaska to Chicago.

On June 13, Judge Frederick A. Smith rendered the decree of the court in favor of Hultberg and the Covenant. The position of Judge Smith was that he had nothing to do with the merits of the controversy unless it could be proved that the award had been vitiated by actual fraud. "In other words, the courts have something else to do than to review a court [the arbitration commission] which the parties have themselves selected."[12]

Judge Smith found that no legal defects appeared in the award or the proceedings connected therewith, that the arbitrators were not guilty of any misbehavior, and that the award was legal, valid, binding, and conclusive. "As to all property rights and the conclusions of said arbitrators thereon, this court, under the evidence herein, refuses to review, modify, or change the same."[13]

---

[12] Manuscript Record, p. 2390. To this view the opposing attorney, John J. Healy, replied, "17 Powers is very good on that question."

[13] *Transcript of Record*, pp. 285 f.

On the matter of costs and expenses, Judge Smith found that Hultberg, Anderson, and Johnson had contributed $4,000 each toward the expenses of the arbitration. Of this sum of $12,000, the arbitrators, had used $5,186.25 for necessary expenses. Of the balance, $6,813.75, Hultberg was entitled to the return of his $4,000, besides $250 from Johnson and $250 from Anderson for costs. Thus, the final balance was $2,313.75, which was to be applied in part payment of the award.

Judge Smith decreed that Hultberg was entitled to payment of $232,200 by Anderson, with interest at five per cent after April 13, 1904. From Johnson, Hultberg was entitled to $23,686.25, with interest at five per cent after April 13, 1904.[14] From the White Star Mining Company of Illinois, Hultberg was entitled to receive the ownership of and title in No. 9 Above.

Thereupon, Judge Smith dismissed the original and amended bills of the White Star Mining Company of Illinois for want of equity. He also dismissed the cross-bills of Johnson and Anderson for want of equity.[15]

At the same time the judge granted the requests for an appeal to the Supreme Court of Illinois. For the White Star Mining Company of Illinois, he set an appeal bond for $125,000; for Claes W. Johnson, $40,000; and for Peter H. Anderson, an appeal bond in the penal sum of $350,000.[16]

---

[14] The original amount awarded was $26,000. Against this sum a credit was allowed of $2,313.75, which was the balance from the arbitrators'funds.

[15] As a result of the award of April 13 by the arbitrators, and of the decision in the Circuit Court of Cook County on June 13, Axel Mellander, secretary of the Covenant, reported: "We have all reason to thank God, that he has led all to a successful conclusion, and that during the proceedings nothing transpired which in the least will throw any shade upon the Covenant. Besides, the Covenant has won respect before all mankind" (*Förbundets Tjugonde Årsmöte i Paxton, Illinois, Rapport till Församlingarna*, p. 86). The events of the next sixteen years seem to be a mockery of Mellander's unrealistic prophecy.

[16] The court decreed that Hultberg was entitled to immediate payment of $6,813.75, which was on deposit with the Merchants' Loan and Trust Company. On April 18, 1904, five days after the arbitrators' award, Hultberg had demanded payment, but the bank refused to honor the checks.

Hultberg's Creditor Bill in the Circuit Court of Cook County (1904-1909)

Successful in his suit by the decree of June 13, 1904, Hultberg sued and prosecuted out of the Circuit Court of Cook County a writ of *fieri facias* on June 15. The writ, directed to the sheriff of Cook County, was returned on June 30, wholly unsatisfied.[17]

On July 1, Hultberg and the Covenant filed their joint creditor's bill. One of the new aspects of this bill was that Mrs. Anderson was made a party defendant along with her husband, Dr. Johnson, and the White Star Mining Company of Illinois.[18] In the original bill of July 1, and in the amended bill of July 15, Hultberg alleged that thirteen separate parties possessed goods or money belonging to Anderson. He further alleged that four other defendants probably possessed money belonging to Anderson. The bill prayed therefore that all seventeen parties be required to divulge what goods they possessed.

Furthermore, the bill alleged that Anderson and his wife had executed a deed of trust to the Chicago Title and Trust Company, conveying the Wilson Avenue apartment to secure a promissory note of $40,000. This note, it was alleged, was taken to hinder and delay the creditors and to convert the building into money more easily concealable. Consequently, the bill prayed that this deed be declared fraudulent and void, and that a receiver be appointed immediately.

Since there was danger that the defendants might take

[17] There was a second execution of the writ on July 25, 1904, and a third on June 12, 1906. All were returned *nulla bona*. Probably on the advice of their attorneys, Mr. and Mrs. P. H. Anderson departed from the jurisdiction of the Illinois and Kansas courts. Unknown to Hultberg, they spent their time in Missouri, Indiana, Wisconsin, and New York, where it was impossible to serve process upon them (United States Circuit Court of Appeals for the Eight Circuit, No. 4837; Frideborg A. Anderson vs. Nels O. Hultberg, *Brief and Argument for Appellee*, pp. 8, 24).

[18] The reason for including Mrs. Anderson was that lots 4 and 5 in H. F. Lundgren's subdivision, besides the apartment building erected thereon, were acquired by her on March 18, 1902; the deed was filed for record as document No. 3219465. This building was located at 904 Wilson Avenue, Chicago (renumbering = 1444 Wilson Avenue).

further steps to convert or conceal their property, the bill prayed also for a writ of injunction.

In response to these prayers, Judge Smith upon an *ex parte* application appointed on the same day—July 1—the Equitable Trust Company as receiver.[19] Further, he granted a writ of injunction, which commanded P. H. Anderson, Frideborg A. Anderson, Claes W. Johnson, Adolph Bernard, and the White Star Mining Company of Illinois to desist from selling, conveying, transferring, or encumbering any property real or personal, directly or indirectly received through the money of P. H. Anderson.

Hultberg and the Covenant filed amendments to the original bill on July 15 and 18. Among the defendants listed were P. H. Anderson, Frideborg A. Anderson, Claes W. Johnson, Adolph Bernard, White Star Mining Company of Illinois, The Chamber of Commerce Safety Vault Company, The Brazilian Diamond, Gold, and Developing Company, The Chicago Title and Trust Company, Axel Chytraus, John J. Healy, Olaf E. Ray, S. G. Cronstedt, The Title Guaranty and Trust Company of Scranton, Pennsylvania. In addition, the amended bill of complaint of July 18 stated that there were grounds for believing that Adolph Lydell, C. A. Bjork, David Nyvall, and C. G. Wilson held property or goods belonging to P. H. Anderson. [20]

On July 19, 1904, Anderson, Johnson, and the White Star Mining Company of Illinois entered their appearance in the

---

[19] The lawyers of Anderson accused Hultberg of purposely bringing his creditor's bill before the same judge—Smith—who had rendered the decree of June 13.

By the appointment of a temporary receiver in July, 1904, Hultberg hoped to prevent the dispersion of the income from the six-flat apartment. On December 4, 1906, Fred Fonda was made receiver and served until his death on April 5, 1911. Thereafter, The Northern Trust Company served as receiver until the final accounting in 1920.

[20] J. A. Hultman's name was added in an amended bill of August 10, 1904. In the original records of this case, No. 253,151, there is an affidavit of J. A. Hultman, filed September 19, 1904, in which he states that he is indebted to P. H. Anderson for $3,000. Naturally, Hultberg was trying to tap every source possible in order to realize as much as possible from his judgment against Anderson.

In 1946, the writer talked with Anderson about some of his debtors. He mentioned without bitterness several men who had never repaid their debts. Let their names remain unmentioned and their memories unsullied!

court, but it was not until August 6, 1907, that Mrs. Anderson filed an answer, and it was not until February 17-18, 1908, that the other defendants filed their answers.[21] On February 21, 1908, Anderson, Johnson, and the White Star Mining Company of Illinois were given permission to file *instanter* a cross-bill, the essential purpose of which was to impeach the decree of June 13, 1904. Accordingly, that same day they filed their plea, entitled, "A Cross-Bill to Establish Unjustness of Decree and for Injunction Restraining Harassing Litigation Thereupon, to Set Aside Decree Lacking in Due Process of Law and in the Nature of a Bill of Review." Mrs. Anderson filed a cross-bill on February 27.

The response of Hultberg and his attorneys was that of presenting to the court a motion on February 28, 1908, to strike the cross-bill from the files, as well as four volumes of exhibits which had been submitted four days earlier. On February 29, Judge Charles M. Walker referred the motion to strike to Sigmund Zeisler, one of the masters of the court. On April 13, 1908, Zeisler made his report. Asserting that the cross-bill was simply a bill of review solely for error apparent upon the face of the decree, which had been affirmed by the Supreme Court of Illinois on April 17, 1906, Zeisler recommended that the motion of Hultberg be granted. Thereupon, on May 28, 1908, Judge Walker approved the master's report and ordered that the cross-bills be stricken from the files. From this order came a motion on May 28 to appeal the issue to the Supreme Court of Illinois. After retaining the prayer for appeal from May 28 to October 2, 1908, Judge Walker issued an order denying the appeal.[22] In the meantime, Mrs. Anderson filed an amended answer on September 9, 1908, to which Hultberg filed exceptions on March 19, 1909. On June 10, 1909, the court sustained the exceptions of Hultberg. Thereupon, the attorneys of Anderson and Johnson

---

[21] A possible reason for this delay was that an appeal to the Supreme Court of Illinois was pending in 1905-1906, and in the United States Supreme Court in 1907.

[22] Manuscript Record, pp. 2650, 2658, 2661-2663. See also Supreme Court of Illinois, No. 7712, Nels O. Hultberg vs. Peter H. Anderson, *Brief and Arguments for Plaintiffs in Error,* p. 131.

filed a praecipe on July 28, 1909, to have the record sent to the Supreme Court of Illinois.[23]

The Appellate Court of Illinois, First District

While the case in the Circuit Court of Cook County was continuing, Anderson, his wife, and Johnson prosecuted an appeal on July 29, 1904, to the Appellate Court of Illinois, First District.[24] This appeal was from the interlocutory order of July 1, issued by Judge Smith, granting an injunction and appointing a receiver.

The record, abstract, and brief were filed by the appellants on August 30, 1904, and on September 13, 1904, the brief of the appellee was filed.

The main arguments presented in the brief for the appellant, Anderson, were as follows:

1. "Equity will not enforce a legal demand until the creditor shall have first exhausted his remedy at law." Hultberg has not exhausted the normal remedies available to him.

2. "No court, judge or master shall grant an injunction without previous notice of the time and place of the application having been given to the defendants to be affected thereby, or such of them as can conveniently be served, unless it shall appear from the bills or affidavit accompanying the same that the rights of the complainant will be unduly prejudiced if the injunction is not issued immediately or without such notice."

3. "The appointment of a receiver without notice is

[23] This case, No. 253,151, lingered on in the Circuit Court of Cook County from 1909 until February 4, 1920, when Judge M. W. Pinckney dismissed Hultberg's creditor's bill. After 1909, the only order found in the records is one of March 14, 1912, giving the defendants additional time to demur, plead, or answer.

[24] In the records of the Appellate Court, these cases are Nos. 11,860 and 11,861; P. H. Anderson and Frideborg A. Anderson, appellants, vs. Nels O. Hultberg et al., appellees; White Star Mining Company, appellant, vs. Nels O. Hultberg et al., appellees. The entries for both cases are identical and are treated as one case.

much more serious than granting an injunction without notice."

4. The Circuit Court of Cook County had no power to grant an injuncttion and appoint a receiver, without notice and without adequate bond, merely because of the fears and apprehensions of the complainant [Hultberg].

5. The most outrageous portion of the injunction is that which prevents Mrs. Anderson from withdrawing money from any bank in this state or elsewhere.

6. The appeals do not have a clear conception of their own position. Their bill [Hultberg's creditor's bill] is one to enforce a trust, to aid an execution, to set aside a fraudulent conveyance, and to stand as a creditor's bill. The bill, therefore, is multifarious and improper.[25]

7. The allegations of the bill are insufficient.

In response to those arguments, the brief of the appellees asserted essentially that their bill stated a case, that it was impossible to serve process on the Andersons because they had departed from the jurisdiction of the court, that the allegations of their bill justified the granting of an injunction and the appointment of a receiver.[26]

Judge Brown listened to oral arguments on October 27 and rendered his opinion on November 28, 1904. Admitting that an interlocutory order entered without notice to the appellants, especially Mrs. Anderson, was the most serious objection, he asserted that the law gave courts discretionary power if they deemed that the rights of the complainant might be unduly prejudiced without immediate action. He took notice of the argument relating to the tying up of the funds of Mrs. Anderson, and asserted that if she could prove that her funds

[25] Appellate Court of Illinois, First District, No. 11,860, P. H. Anderson and Frideborg A. Anderson vs. Nels O. Hultberg *et al.*, *Brief for Appellants*, pp. 8, 9, 12, 15.

[26] *Ibid.*, *Brief and Argument for Appellees, Nels O. Hultberg and the Swedish Evangelical Mission Covenant of America*, pp. 3, 8, 16, 17, 23.

were independent of those of her husband, she was entitled to relief. The judge then pointed out that an interlocutory order merely preserves the status quo, that only temporary inconveniences can result from the granting of an injunction and the appointment of a receiver. Denying the assertion that the allegations of the complainant's bill were insufficient, he supported their sufficiency to justify the interlocutory order for an injunction and receivership. Consequently, he affirmed the decision of the lower court. A petition for rehearing was filed on December 8, 1904, and denied on December 12.[27]

Mrs. Anderson appealed a second time to the Appellate Court of Illinois in 1908. In February of that year, the Circuit Court of Cook County was threatening to enter judgment against her if she did not make her appearance. Consequently, on February 27, 1908, she filed her cross-bill, in which she alleged that her defense in the District Court of the United States for the District of Kansas was the same as the defense in the Circuit Court of Cook County. To carry on two identical defense suits at the same time, she said, would involve double expense. Therefore, she asked for a temporary injunction restraining Hultberg from prosecuting his suit in Kansas until the original bill had been heard in the Circuit Court of Cook County.

This motion for a temporary injunction was referred to a master, who made some special recommendations which were acceptable to the court. Thereupon, an order was entered with the stipulation that the motion for a temporary injunction be granted, subject to two conditions. One was that Hultberg be restrained from prosecuting that part of the bill which pertained to the lands in Dickinson County, Kansas. The second was that the temporary injunction would be vacated and annulled unless Mrs. Anderson delivered to the Chicago Title and Trust Company on or before March 18, 1908, a deed properly executed, conveying to the said Chicago Title and Trust Company, as trustee, the lands in Dickinson County, Kansas, to be held by the court and subject to the final disposition as may be made by the court when the hearing on

---

[27] P. H. Anderson vs. N. O. Hultberg, 117 Illinois Appellate, 231-247.

the original bill is completed. These provisions did not please Mrs. Anderson, and therefore she perfected her appeal from this temporary conditional injunction to the Appellate Court of Illinois, First District. The appellees moved to dismiss this appeal on the ground that the order of the Circuit Court of Cook County was not appealable. On November 12, 1908, the appellee's motion to dismiss the bill was sustained and the appeal dismissed. On November 30, 1908, an appeal for rehearing was denied.[28]

The District Court of Dickinson County of the Eighth Judicial District, Kansas

Encouraged by the arbitration award of April 13, 1904, and by the decree of the Circuit Court of Cook County, June 13, 1904, Hultberg brought a suit of attachment in the District Court of Dickinson County, Abilene, Kansas, on June 20, 1904.[29] The purpose of this lawsuit was to secure possession of farm lands in Dickinson County, Kansas, on the theory that they had been purchased by Anderson from money which came from No. 9 Above in 1899, and which constituted therefore trust funds subject to the judgment of $232,200. Hultberg charged that Anderson had property and possessions in Kansas worth about $90,000.[30]

On December 26, 1899, Mrs. Anderson had obtained a warranty deed for a farm of 960 acres in sections 15 and 22, township 14, known as the Hafner land. The consideration was $12,500. On April 1, 1901, Gustaf and Hannah Alstrom had conveyed a deed to Mrs. Anderson for land approximating 232 acres in sections 2 and 3, township 14, known as the Alstrom land. The consideration was $6,000.[31] Hultberg claimed

---

[28] Frideborg A. Anderson vs. N. O. Hultberg, 144 Illinois Appellate, 533. See also United States Circuit Court of Appeals, No. 4837, Frideborg A. Anderson vs. Nels O. Hultberg, *Brief and Argument for Appellee*, p. 27.

[29] Nels O. Hultberg vs. P. H. Anderson *et al.*, No. 4332. In this suit the attorneys for Hultberg were E. C. Little, C. E. Rugh, and David Ritchie. Anderson's lawyers were S. S. Smith and G. W. Hurd.

[30] This estimate is fairly accurate. The valuation and appraisement of six parcels of property on which Sheriff J. W. Baker levied a writ of attachment was $33,476. Besides, Anderson had given $25,000 to Walden College, of McPherson, Kansas. In addition, he probably had notes, mortgages, possessions, or money approximating $30,000.

121

that the purchase money for these farms came from No. 9 Above, and therefore belonged to him, but Mrs. Anderson contended that the money had come from No. 2 Above. Therefore, regardless of the question as to who owned No. 9 Above, she said, the farms belonged to her.[32]

In addition to this suit of attachment, which in effect was a creditor's bill, Hultberg instituted garnishment proceedings against twelve defendants, whom he caused to be summoned as garnishees. These were: The School Association of the Swedish Evangelical Mission Conference of Kansas, The McPherson Bank, The Swedish-German State Bank, The Citizens' State Bank, The Peoples' State Bank, The Farmers' and Merchants' Bank [all these banks were in McPherson], C. P. Peterson of Enterprise, G. E. H. Peterson of Enterprise, Peterson Brothers [the previous two men as a partnership in Enterprise], Andrew Beckstrom of Lindsborg, Oscar Elvin of Lindsborg, and Jacob Peterson of Lindsborg. According to Hultberg, these garnishees held money or property of the Andersons, under some special agreement with Nels Peterson, David Nyvall, and S. Oscar Lindgren, who in turn claimed that their money or property was to be donated to The School Association of the Swedish Evangelical Mission Conference of Kansas.[33] During July and August, 1904, these defendants filed their answers, denying that they were indebted in any manner to Peter or Frideborg Anderson.[34]

[31] The Hafner deed was recorded on January 8, 1900, the Alstrom deed on April 15, 1901, in the office of the Registrar of Deeds of Dickinson County, Kansas.

[32] On this point Hultberg's lawyers were able to prove that although the farms stood in the name of Mrs. Anderson, yet the drafts paid by John R. Anderson and Albert E. Anderson, renters of the farms, were sent to Mr. Anderson. These drafts had been unearthed after a twenty-hour search by the officers of the Dickinson County Bank.

[33] Circuit Court of the United States, District of Kansas, First Division, No. 8609, Nels O. Hultberg vs. P. H. Anderson *et al., Bill in Equity,* pp. 22-26.

[34] Oscar Elvin admitted in his answer of July 28, 1904, that he was indebted to Frideborg A. Anderson for $1,500. In a further reply of August 26, he said he had examined the records and found he had no indebtedness. In 1901, he had borrowed $2,000 from Frideborg A. Anderson. By 1904, he still owed $1,500, but since Mrs. Anderson had assigned the note to The School Association of the Swedish Evangelical Mission Conference of Kansas, Elvin no longer had any indebtedness, so far as Mrs. Anderson was concerned. But he did owe The School Association, and this debt Hultberg regarded as owing to him.

During 1904, very little was accomplished in court. The sheriff, J. W. Baker, duly executed the writ of attachment on six parcels of land, including the Hafner and Alstrom farms, and the garnishees filed their negative answers. Since it was impossible to serve process on P. H. Anderon and his wife personally, as non-residents of Kansas, resort to public notice in *The Abilene Daily Chronicle* was made by commanding them to appear in court by August 22, 1904.[35] Despite this fact, Anderson and his wife did not appear, but their attorneys on January 26, 1905, moved the court to require Hultberg to state and number his causes of action separately. Since this motion was sustained, Hultberg found it necessary to file on March 20, 1905, an amended bill. To this amended bill, Anderson and his wife filed demurrers on April 3, 1905. Hearings were held in court on May 16 and 18 as a result of which Anderson's demurrer was overruled, but Mrs. Anderson's demurrer was sustained on both counts of defect of parties defendant and misjoinder of parties defendant. Thereupon, with the permission of the court, Hultberg filed an amended petition *instanter* on May 18, 1905, against P. H. Anderson alone, to which Anderson filed an answer on June 10, 1905.[36]

During 1906, issues were not joined because of the prosecution of another suit in the Supreme Court of Illinois, but when this suit was carried to the Supreme Court of the United States, Anderson was not able to stay proceedings any longer in the Kansas case. On January 28, 1907, he moved the court to vacate the order of attachment issued on June 20, 1904. In this he was unsuccessful, and on January 31, 1907, Judge O. L. Moore decreed that Hultberg should have judgment against Anderson for $264,708.[37]

As a result of this judgment, a writ of execution was issued to sheriff John B. Favor on February 1, whereby two small

[35] Proof of publication was filed in the court on August 22, 1904.

[36] The reason for Mrs. Anderson's successful demurrer was that Hultberg had filed his judgment as though it applied to both Anderson and his wife. The Circuit Court of Cook County, however, had given a judgment against Anderson only.

[37] This sum included the original judgment for $232,200, besides five per cent interest of $32,508 for a period of two years, nine months, and eighteen days—April 13, 1904, to January 31, 1907.

parcels of land, standing in the name of P. H. Anderson, were sold at public sale. By this sale, Hultberg realized $3,300. An *alias* execution of March 11, and a *pluries* execution of July 13, 1907, were returned by the sheriff, with the endorsement: "I am unable to find property belonging to the within named defendant on which to levy this writ."[38]

Hultberg's victory in court was not conclusive. He had been unable to subject the property or funds of the garnishee defendants, and he was unable to include Mrs. Anderson's property within the scope of the judgment. As a matter of fact, Mrs. Anderson applied to the court on September 7, 1912, for a motion to have an order entered *nunc pro tunc*, in her favor, on the basis of her successful demurrer of May 16, 1905. The court had no alternative, and on September 9, 1912, Judge R. L. King ordered that Mrs. Anderson have and recover from Hultberg payment for her costs of $176.25, and that execution issue therefor.[39] On October 2, 1913, it was finally ordered that the case "be and the same is hereby dismissed for want of prosecution."[40]

The Supreme Court of Illinois
(1904-1906)

While Hultberg was prosecuting his suit in Kansas, and while an appeal was being adjudicated in the Appellate Court of Illinois, another appeal was made to the Supreme Court of Illinois.

When Judge Smith made his decision on June 13, 1904, Anderson, Johnson, and the White Star Mining Company of Illinois prayed for and obtained separate appeals from this decision. Only the White Star Mining Company of Illinois, however, perfected its appeal, although Anderson and Johnson did file cross-errors.

[38] The third execution was returned August 3, 1907. At the public sale, held on March 11, 1907, Hultberg bid $3,300, a sum which was applied to his judgment.

[39] Original records in the office of the clerk of the court at Abilene, Kansas. No. 4332.

[40] Journal entry in court records, filed October 23, 1913.

From the twenty-nine errors assigned, we may extract the following as being the most significant:

1. "That the arbitrators erred in the conclusions of law and fact upon which they based their award, and their award was contrary to the law and the evidence."

2. "That the submission agreement was not binding upon the appellant, because Johnson, when he executed it, had no authority to do so."

3. "That Hultberg's claim was founded in maintenance and was therefore unlawful and void."

4. "That the arbitrators made their award without taking or requiring any accounting."

5. "That the disposition made of the $6,813.75 on deposit in the Merchants' Loan and Trust Company was unauthorized."

6. "That the award ought not to have been enforced by the court but, on the contrary, should have been set aside and annulled."

7. That the submission was special and not general, and therefore subject to review.

8. That an express trust cannot be established by parole proof.[41]

Although the praecipe, abstract, and briefs were filed in October, 1904, it was not until October 24, 1905, that the court rendered its decision in favor of Hultberg. The court took the view that the decision of the arbitrators was final and conclusive. It said that an arbitration commission was a mode of settling disputes which should receive every encouragement from courts of equity. "A contrary course would be substitution of the judgment of the chancellor in place of the judges chosen by the parties, and would make an award the commencement—not the end—of litigation." The court further

---

[41] Supreme Court of Illinois, No. 3912; White Star Mining Company, appellant, vs. Nels O. Hultberg, *Statement of the Case . . .,* p. 36. See further Circuit Court of the United States, Northern District of Illinois, Eastern Division. Peter H. Anderson *et al.* vs. The Swedish Evangelical Mission Covenant of America, *Exhibits,* pp. 49-60. See also 220 Illinois 578.

decided that the submission was general, not special, that the award was within the submision, and that there was no fraud or mistake of law or fact appearing upon the face of it. Therefore, it said that there was no theory of law by which a court of equity could set aside the decision of the arbitrators. All questions settled by them were *res judicata*. "The chancellor who heard the cause in the court below decided it correctly, and the decree will be affirmed."[42]

Despite the strong opinion of the court, a rehearing was granted in December, 1905, and on April 17, 1906, a second affirmance was made. In this opinion five of the justices were for affirmance, but two, including Chief Justice J. H. Cartwright, entered their dissent, asserting that injustice and fraud had been worked upon the appellant.[43] On May 11, 1906, a petition was filed for a rehearing as to the opinion of affirmance, but upon motion of the defendant this petition was stricken from the files on June 13, 1906.[44]

The second affirmance of April 17, 1906, was a result of Judge Smith's decree of June 13, 1904 (case No. 251,594). On the basis of this decree, Hultberg filed a creditor's bill on July 1, 1904, in the Circuit Court of Cook County (case No. 253,151). When Judge Walker sustained a motion on May 28, 1908, to strike the cross-bill of the defendants, Anderson, Johnson, and the White Star Mining Company appealed a second time to the Supreme Court of Illinois. They filed their bill on December 21, 1911, and the Supreme Court on February 24, 1912, affirmed the order of the Circuit Court of Cook County. A petition for rehearing was denied.

[42] Supreme Court of Illinois, No. 3912; White Star Mining Company of Illinois vs. Nels O. Hultberg *et al., Appendix to Petition for Rehearing,* p. 44.

[43] Supreme Court of Illinois, No. 7712; Nels O. Hultberg *et al.* vs. P. H. Anderson *et al., Brief and Argument for Defendants in Error,* pp. 5 f. The five judges who voted for affirmance were Carroll C. Boggs, Benjamin D. Magruder, James B. Ricks, Guy C. Scott, and Jacob Wilkin. The two dissenting judges were James H. Cartwright and John P. Hand. See United States Circuit Court of Appeals for the Eighth Circuit, No. 4837; Frideborg A. Anderson, appellant vs. Nels O. Hultberg, appellee, *Transcript of Record,* pp. 282-333.

[44] On December 17, 1907, the White Star Mining Company of Illinois filed its "Petition for Leave to File Additional Petition for Rehearing," but the court denied the petition.

From this order of affirmance, Anderson, Hultberg, and the White Star Mining Company appealed to the Supreme Court of the United States. Once more their writ of error was dismissed, February 23, 1915.[45]

The Supreme Court of the United States (1906-1907)

As a result of the decisions in the Supreme Court of Illinois, the White Star Mining Company of Illinois applied on June 22, 1906, for a writ of error from the Supreme Court of the United States. That writ was also made a supersedeas. Anderson and Johnson also procured writs of error, but these were not made supersedeas. The writs were allowed on February 9, 1907, the record was filed in Washington on March 11, and on April 22, a motion was made by Hultberg and the Covenant that the writs of error be dismissed. On April 29, 1907, the motion was granted and the writs of error were dismissed on the ground that the Supreme Court of the United States was without jurisdiction in the case. On May 27, 1907, a petition for rehearing was denied, and on May 31, 1907, mandates were issued by the clerk of the court.[46]

As a consequence of this decision, the Chicago Title and Trust Company delivered fifty Swedish bonds to Charles D. Hamill, attorney of record for the White Star Mining Company of Illinois, with the understanding that the proceeds therefrom should be applied against the judgment of $26,000. By July 26, 1907, the judgment had been satisfied. Another consequence of the decision in the Supreme Court of the United States was that Hultberg decided to go to Alaska in the summer of 1907 in order to begin work anew on "his" mine, No. 9 Above.[47]

[45] Supreme Court of Illinois, No. 7712; P. H. Anderson, *et al.,* vs. Nels O. Hultberg *et al., Reply for Plaintiffs in Error, passim.* See also 238 U. S. 605 f. A previous dismissal was made on April 29, 1907. See *infra.*

[46] 205 U. S. 541, mem. *Svenska Evangeliska Missionsförbundets i Amerika Årsberättelse för dess 23dje Verksamhetsår, 1906-1907* (Chicago, 1907) p. 26.

[47] Circuit Court of the United States, Northern District of Illinois; Peter H. Anderson *et al.* vs. The Swedish Evangelical Mission Covenant of America, *Bill in Equity,* pp. 21, 74-77. Between 1907 and 1910, Hultberg was said to have obtained $50,000 from No. 9 Above (*Ibid.* p. 77).

The Circuit Court of the United States, Northern District of Illinois, Eastern Division

One of the statements made by a dissenting justice of the Supreme Court of Illinois was that "plaintiffs in error have never as yet had a hearing upon the merits in this case." This statement was true, since the courts uniformly took the position that they should not sit in review upon the findings of the arbitration commission.

Hoping to secure a review of the merits of the case in a federal court, Anderson in 1910 filed a bill in equity in the Circuit Court of the United States, Northern District of Illinois, Eastern Division. He included the affirming and dissenting opinions of the Supreme Court of Illinois as a part of his bill of complaint. Three separate demurrers were filed, which set up that "enough does not appear in the bill to show jurisdiction in the court; that the court has no jurisdiction to hear the subject-matter; that the matters and things and questions and demands, concerning which relief is prayed, have already been adjudicated; that complainants are not entitled to the relief prayed for, or any part thereof; and that the bill of complaint is wholly without equity."[48] The demurrers were sustained, and the bill was dismissed for want of equity and jurisdiction.

The Supreme Court of the United States (1912-1914)

On October 31, 1912, Anderson, his wife, Dr. Johnson, and the White Star Mining Company of Illinois prayed for and were allowed an appeal to the Supreme Court of the United States from the order of dismissal. The appellants were allowed a direct appeal because the cause involved the application of the United States constitution. In their bill, the appellants contended that the procedure of the state courts was repugnant to the constitution of the United States because such procedure involved a denial of equal protection of the laws, of

[48] Supreme Court of the United States, No. 374; Peter H. Anderson *et al.* vs. Swedish Evangelical Mission Covenant of America *et al.*, *Brief for Appellants*, pp. 1 f.

due process of law, and of privileges and immunities of American citizens, as well as the abrogation of the liberty of contract.[49]

After briefs had been filed on both sides, the case was argued orally before the court, and on November 30, 1914, the Supreme Court of the United States affirmed the order of dismissal of the lower court, and dismissed the appeal for want of equity and jurisdiction. A petition for rehearing was denied.[50]

The District Court of the United States for the District of Kansas, First Division (1907-1916)

In order to attack the property and possessions of defendants outside of Dickinson County, Hultberg began suit on September 7, 1907, at Topeka in the District Court of the United States for the District of Kansas. Among the thirty-two defendants were the twelve named in the previous suit at Abilene. Besides Anderson and his wife, there were nine relatives: Andrew J. and Matilda C. Anderson (his father and mother); Andrew G. and Jennie K. Anderson (his brother and sister-in-law); John R. and Albert Anderson (his brothers); Maggie Anderson Hjelm and Nellie Anderson Hanson (sisters); and Oscar Hanson (brother-in-law). Besides these there were Nels Peterson, David Nyvall, and S. Oscar Lindgren of McPherson; Charles and Matilda Hanson and Ernest Linde of Dickinson County; E. P. Liljestrom of Lindsborg; and Annie Peterson and Minnie Peterson of Enterprise.

The separate pleas, disclaimers, or demurrers filed by the defendants consumed many months for their preparation and hearing. Those pleas based on the statute of limitations were denied. To those demurrers which claimed want of equity because Hultberg had adequate remedy at law in a state court, Judge John C. Pollock replied that since Hultberg had proceeded as far as possible with his former suit in the District Court of Dickinson County, he was justified in seeking remedy in a federal court. Consequently, such demurrers were overruled. To those demurrers which charged multifariousness,

49 *Ibid.,* pp. 30-63.
50 205 U. S. 540; 235 U. S. 692.

Judge Pollock ruled that although the judgment debtor was found in the hands of many people, the object and scope of the bill of complaint tended toward a single result. Hence the purpose of the bill was not multifarious.

In the case of Anderson and his wife, the court found it impossible to serve them personally, inasmuch as they kept out of reach by various means. Being non-residents of Kansas, they were brought in by constructive notice, and when they failed to make their appearance, a decree *pro confesso* was entered against them on November 23, 1908, by Judge John F. Philips.[51] Two days later Mrs. Anderson filed her answer, in which she questioned the appeal to a federal court and denied its jurisdiction. When Hultberg moved that this plea be stricken because it was late, defective, and unsupported by affidavit, the court gave Mrs. Anderson leave to file an amended plea *instanter*, and she did so on December 17, 1908. On January 19, 1909, permission was given by the court to vacate the decree *pro confesso* of November 23, 1908, so far as Mrs. Anderson was concerned.

During 1909 and 1910, answers, exceptions, amendments, exceptions to amendments, and Hultberg's replication were filed, and modified, sustained or overruled. Therefore, it was not until October 24, 1911, that the cause was finally put to issue. Judge Pollock on November 6 appointed William Needles of Kansas City, Kansas, as special examiner. Needles came to Chicago in August, 1912, to take testimony. Among those subpoenaed were Mrs. S. G. Cronstedt, Otto Hogfeldt, David Nyvall, Axel Chytraus, Van Buren Powers, Edward A. Schroeder, and John W. Behee.[52]

---

[51] A notice directing Anderson and his wife to appear was published for six consecutive weeks in the *Abilene Weekly Chronicle,* December 18, 1907-January 22, 1908. Attorney Harris F. Williams on December 14, placed two certified copies of the notice beneath the door leading to Anderson's apartment in Chicago. Mrs. Hellstrom, the housekeeper, lived there, but she was evidently instructed not to reveal the whereabouts of the Andersons.

[52] Mrs. Cronstedt, Nyvall, and Chytraus were questioned on the whereabouts of Anderson; Hogfeldt was asked about the student days of Mrs. Anderson; Powers, who was a clerk in the Chamber of Commerce Safety Vaults, was questioned about Anderson's box there; Schroeder, an auditor in the State Bank of Chicago, was asked about Anderson's bank deposits; and Behee, a neighbor of Anderson, was questioned about his watching the apartment of Anderson—as he had been instructed to do by H. F. Williams, Hultberg's lawyer!

An unexpected complication developed during Needles' visit to Chicago. Since the examiner desired to know the whereabouts of Anderson, he asked this question of Nyvall, Mrs. Cronstedt, and Chytraus. Nyvall didn't know, Mrs. Cronstedt refused to divulge the answer because of the advice of her attorney, Chytraus, and Chytraus himself flatly refused.[53]

Thereupon, Hultberg's lawyers took the matter to the District Court of the United States for the Northern District. Arguments were made before Judge Christian C. Kohlsaat on August 15, 1912, and on August 27, Chytraus was ordered to answer the question of the examiner. On September 16, Chytraus once more refused to tell the examiner where Anderson could be found, and as a result was ordered to appear before the court on October 1, to show cause why he should not be punished for contempt of court. Chytraus argued that the examiner had no authority in Illinois, that the court was without jurisdiction to entertain an application without the facts, that Anderson's address was still the same as it had been for the last ten years, and that he had a right to safeguard his client by not divulging privileged communications.

On October 22, the court rendered its decree. It said that divulging an address is not "privileged communication," that the court did not err in its order of August 27, and that Chytraus could not refrain from answering because he was one of Anderson's lawyers. Paradoxically, the court concluded by saying that it had no power or right to punish Chytraus for his failure to comply, and therefore it dismissed Hultberg's petition at the cost of the petitioner.

Stung by this peculiar decision, Hultberg carried the matter to the United States Circuit Court of Appeals, Seventh Circuit, in February, 1913. At first the court refused to accept the motion of Chytraus to dismiss the appeal, but on November 21, 1913, the court did dismiss the appeal. The net result was that Hultberg was not able to summon Anderson and obtain his testimony, either by examiner or by oral hearing in court.[54]

---

[53] United States Circuit Court of Appeals, Eighth Circuit, No. 4837; Frideborg A. Anderson vs. Nels O. Hultberg, *Transcript of Record,* pp. 383-393.

[54] 203 Fed. 853; 214 Fed. 349.

Shortly after these contempt of court proceedings had begun, the examiner, William Needles, died on November 17, 1912. His successor was John E. McFadden of Kansas City, Kansas, who continued to take testimony in Missouri and Kansas in 1913. On the basis of this testimony, the court appointed J. R. Harrison, U. S. Marshall, as received for the Hafner and Alstrom farms, owned by Mrs. Anderson.

The issues were finally brought to trial on April 1 and 2, 1915, before Judge Pollock at Kansas City, Kansas, and on April 3, the case was submitted. A whole year elapsed before the decision of the court was filed on April 1, 1916, and on May 20, 1916, the decree was rendered in favor of Hultberg. Mrs. Anderson filed an appeal on June 26, 1916.

The United States Circuit Court of Appeals for the Eighth Circuit

In her assignment of errors, Mrs. Anderson said that the District Court of the United States for the District of Kansas erred in sustaining the exceptions of Hultberg of May 9, 1910, and May 29, 1911; that the court erred in appointing a receiver for her property; that the court erred in regarding the decrees of January 31, 1907, and of June 13, 1904, as establishing any facts relevant to her; and that the court erred by not finding that her farms had been purchased from money obtained from No. 2 Above rather than from No. 9 Above.

On January 7, 1918, the opinion of the court was filed. Justice Walter H. Sanborn, who delivered the opinion of the court, held that an appeal in a suit of equity in the national courts invoked a new hearing and decision on the merits of the case. Going behind the arbitration award and the decree of the Circuit Court of Cook County, he concluded that the evidence for any kind of trust relationship between Anderson and the Covenant was "so weak as to be almost negligible." Therefore, if the Covenant was not a creditor of Anderson in 1899 and 1901, when Mrs. Anderson acquired the Hafner and Alstrom farms, neither the Covenant nor its assignee, Hultberg, had any right to those lands. "Let the decree below [District

132

Court of the United States for the District of Kansas] be reversed with costs against the appellee [Hultberg] and let this case be remanded to the court below for further proceedings not inconsistent with the views expressed in this opinion." [55]

This opinion completely upset all the previous decisions during the past fourteen years. Hultberg filed a petition for a rehearing, but the court denied the petition on September 2, 1918, and reaffirmed the decision. Hultberg then petitioned the Supreme Court of the United States for a writ of certiorari, and supported the petition with a lengthy brief. On December 16, 1918, the petition was denied, and a petition for rehearing was also denied on March 3, 1919.

During 1919, the final settlement was worked out, and on February 2, 1920, an agreement was signed. By the terms, the report of the Northern Trust Company, as receiver, was accepted. This report revealed a balance of $28,361.53, of which $15,000 was given to Hultberg and the Covenant and $13,361.53 to Anderson. The apartment building in Chicago was returned to Mrs. Anderson, the receivers for the building and the farms in Kansas were discharged. The notes and other evidences regarding the indebtedness of the Denver Church, of Adolph Lydell, Swanson, and J. A. Hultman were given to the Covenant for the purpose of settling the claims.[56] The original decree against Anderson was deemed satisfied, and the bill of complaint was dismissed without costs on February 4, 1920. Judge M. W. Pinckney issued a final order on February 20, 1920, discharging the case.

---

[55] 247 Fed. 273; 159 C. C. A. 367. Justice Sanborn, who delivered the opinion, was one of the keenest legal minds in the country. His published decisions numbered approximately 1500, of which 1370 appeared in the *Federal Reporter.* This record "has probably not been equalled in the history of our country" (*In Memoriam—Walter H. Sanborn, 1845-1928*).

[56] Protokollen, 1917-1921, of Sub-Committee, Meeting of February 2, 1920, pp. 141 f. These manuscript minutes are in the Covenant Archives.

PART V—1898-1920

RAMIFICATIONS AND CONCLUSIONS

RAMIFICATIONS AND CONCLUSIONS

In our story of No. 9 Above, we have thus far related its history in four main sections. Part I included an account of the discovery of gold, the first mining season of 1899, the great stampede of 1900, and the emergence of diverse points of view by P. H. Anderson and the Covenant regarding the ownership of No. 9 Above. Part II was the story of the Eskimo lawsuit, as well as of the increasing tension between Anderson, on one side, and Hultberg and the Covenant officials on the other side. The result of this tension was the decision of the Covenant executive committee and of the annual conference to assign their claim of ownership to Hultberg. Missionary Hultberg recorded his claim of ownership in Nome, presented his demand for control of the mine, and in consequence of this demand signed articles of agreement to arbitrate the matter. Part III was a narration of the hearings held before the arbitration commission, together with the testimony given on each side and the award made by the arbitrators in favor of Hultberg. In consequence of this award, the dispute was carried to the courts. The history of the prolonged litigation from 1904 to 1919 constituted the substance of Part IV.

Before ending our discussion, we need to indicate what were the wider ramifications of this story, and we feel an obligation to express some conclusions on the story itself. The majesty of fact may indeed be lofty, imposing and exalted, but we need to remember that facts without interpretation and significance tend to be lifeless and barren. As Kant expressed it, percepts without concepts are blind, and concepts without percepts are empty.

Although the story of No. 9 Above has been related as a single isolated account, it must be remembered that No. 9 was only one claim among some five thousand which were staked.[1] Of these, several hundred claims were involved in bitter litigation, the history of which somewhat parallels that of No. 9 Above in its non-ecclesiastical aspects. Moreover, Anderson and his mines were an integral part of the discovery of gold throughout northwestern Alaska, of the establishment of Nome, and of the transition of this mining camp into a civilized community and a supply depot for the Seward Peninsula and the northernmost communities up to Point Barrow.[2]

Furthermore, No. 9 Above is a part of one of the most treacherous schemes ever conceived to swindle owners of their hard-won gains by legal means. The story of the Noyes-McKenzie conspiracy is as fascinating in its bold plans as it is unbelievable in its diabolical implementation. After Congress had enacted its legislation for Alaska,—"An Act Making Further Provision for Civil Government for Alaska and for Other Purposes," which became law on June 6, 1900,—the newly appointed judge, Arthur H. Noyes, proceeded immediately to Nome, landed on July 21, and two days later appointed his friend Alexander McKenzie as receiver of six of the richest properties on Anvil Creek, one of which belonged to Anderson. This *ex-parte* proceeding, done in chambers before court had been opened and before any papers had been filed with the clerk of the court, was as unjust as it was unprecedented. When the legal owners filed their bill of exceptions, Judge Noyes dismissed their appeal and broadened the powers of the receiver. Judge Noyes even denied the plaintiff's petition for an appeal, but notwithstanding the case was carried to the United States Circuit Court of Appeals for the Ninth Circuit, in San Francisco. Receiver McKenzie refused to obey the writ of supersedeas issued by the appellate court, and assumed that his

[1] For general information on the mines, see Sam C. Dunham, "The Yukon and Nome Gold Regions," *Bulletin of the Department of Labor*, V (July, 1900) ; see also Eugene McElwaine, *The Truth About Alaska, the Golden Land of the Midnight Sun* (Chicago, 1901).

[2] See three articles by Leland H. Carlson, "The Discovery of Gold at Nome, Alaska," *The Pacific Historical Review*, September, 1946; "The First Mining Season at Nome, Alaska—1899," *The Pacific Historical Review*, May, 1947; and "Nome: From Mining Camp to Civilized Community," *Pacific Northwest Quarterly*, July, 1947.

political influence was strong enough to enable him to circumvent the law. As Republican state chairman of North Dakota, as the power that had sent members to Congress, and as an intimate friend of Mark Hanna, senator from Ohio and Republican national chairman, McKenzie was certain that his political connections were strong enough to protect him. To his surprise, his appeals to the Supreme Court of the United States for a writ of habeas corpus and a writ of certiorari were denied. Thereupon, the case was tried in San Francisco, and in February, 1901, McKenzie was sentenced for contempt of court to one year's imprisonment in the Alameda County jail. In the fall of the same year, Judge Noyes was tried on the same charge, found guilty and sentenced to pay a fine of $1000. Thereupon, the U. S. Senate took cognizance of the proceedings in the Alaska Court, and the attorney general of the United States decided to investigate the broader charges against Judge Noyes. As a consequence of this investigation, the attorney general recommended to the president of the United States the removal of the judge from his territorial position, and Theodore Roosevelt dismissed Noyes from office on February 24, 1902.[3]

The ramifications of No. 9 Above in the Covenant at large were numerous and widespread. The entire denomination was divided into two hostile camps. Members of the Covenant executive committee were almost unanimous in their opposition to Anderson, but divergent in the intensity of their beliefs about Anderson's guilt. States like Kansas and Illinois disagreed in their attitudes and expressed their respective views in denominational and sectional publications.[4] Some churches took definite stands on the issues, but in other congregations individuals held

---

[3] For McKenzie, see manuscript material in the office of the clerk of the court, United States Circuit Court of Appeals for the Seventh Circuit (San Francisco), Cases No. 632, 634, 636, 701, 702, 703, 744. See also National Archives, Department of Justice, File 10,000/1900, and Office of the Pardon Attorney, Record U, McKenzie. For Noyes, see National Archives, Department of Justice, File No. 10,000/1900, Appointment Files; Department of Justice, Judges and Clerks, U. S. Courts, Nos. 21, 22. See also the pamphlet, *The Case of Judge Arthur H. Noyes of Nome, Alaska,* in the Department of Justice, File 10,000/1900.

[4] A good example of a sectional publication was the pamphlet issued in 1903 by N. Peterson and S. O. Lindgren, *Förbundets Komite och P. H. Anderson.* This pamphlet caused the Covenant to demand an apology from the authors, and, if not forthcoming, to strike their names from the Covenant's roll.

opposite convictions. Relatives and friends of such participants as Anderson, Carlson, Högfeldt, Lindgren, Mellander, Nyvall, and Petterson became involved in the struggle. Cleavages were apparent in boards and committees, and resignations from churches were not unknown. Bitter feelings and passionate exhortations were particularly characteristic of the annual conferences held in 1903 at Minneapolis and in 1904 at Paxton. The closed sessions held at Minneapolis, the entire morning's speech by Mellander, the resignation of Nyvall as secretary of the Covenant, the *argumentum ad hominem*, and the consultations with a law firm sufficiently attest to the intensity of conviction. The conference at Paxton in 1904 was carried on in an atmosphere even more charged than that of 1903. General charges and specific accusations were met by recriminations and counter-arguments. Innuendos, veiled insinuations, and even open insults were used by some of the speakers, whose emotions had outrun their rational judgments. After making a most insulting statement, one delegate was curtly told to sit down.[5]

Another ramification of the disputes on the ownership of the Alaskan gold mine was the effect upon North Park College. Anderson's donation of $29,000 to the school made possible the building of a boy's dormitory and a home for President Nyvall in 1902. As a consequence, Nyvall was accused of sympathy for Anderson because of his benefiting personally from the donation. Nyvall found it necessary to write an article in which he explained that he paid rent to the college for his home as any other tenant did.[6] Even more appalling was the widening rift between Mellander and Nyvall, both professors in the theological seminary. The real reason for the breach was the diametrically opposite views of the two men on Anderson. Mellander was in full sympathy with Petterson, Högfeldt, and the newspaper *Missions-Vännen* in their animosity to Anderson. In 1901, Mellander had received a free trip to Palestine, paid

[5] Manuscript Minutes of the three sessions held June 25, 1904. See also *Förbundets Årsmöte i Minneapolis, Minn., Rapport till Församlingarna, 1903* (Chicago, 1903), pp.148-152.

[6] Minutes of Sub-Committee, 1901-04, January 7, 1902. The article is in *Missions-Vännen*, February 4, 1902, p. 5.

for by Alaskan gold which missionary Karlson had extracted from his holdings near Council City and Nome. In 1902, he had taken the lead in pushing charges of immoral conduct against Anderson, and had expressed these charges in a printed article in the official Covenant publication, the *Missionären*. At the annual meeting in June, 1903, Mellander had made an all-morning speech replete with documentary evidence, charges, and denunciations against Anderson. As the leader with Petterson in prosecuting charges, Mellander naturally disagreed sharply with Nyvall's views.

To this basic difference may be added the divergence in their views on school policy. Mellander believed in the strict, literal, disciplinarian philosophy of education whereas Nyvall advocated a lenient, liberal, interest-motivating educational policy. As a brilliant teacher and speaker, Nyvall undoubtedly possessed an intrinsic distaste for any hickory-stick, rote form of pedagogy. The men also disagreed in their general attitude toward amusements, recreation, clubs, social activities, plays, and "worldly" practices, Nyvall interpreting the religious constitution liberally and broadly, as a "loose-constructionist," Mellander interpreting the Biblical injunctions literally and narrowly, as a "strict-constructionist." This latter difference was minor, but the Alaskan difference was major. It is no wonder, therefore, that the smoldering embers of disagreement flared up into scorching flames as the Alaskan winds fanned the fuel. Strengthened in the justness of his cause by two court victories which had been won during the previous two months,[7] Mellander charged Nyvall with maladministration, weak enforcement of discipline, educational laxity, and favoritism to one who had defrauded the Covenant. Mellander further declared that since he could not work with Nyvall any longer, so long as the latter held such differing views, he felt it imperative to resign. Fortunately, Nyvall's friends were quick to defend him, and Nyvall himself moved that Mellander's resignation should not be accepted. The two men shook hands, and the session ended dramatically.

[7] These victories were the award of the arbitration commission on April 13, 1904, and the decision of the Circuit Court of Cook County on June 13, 1904.

The settlement of the difficulties at Paxton resulted in Mellander's decision to continue his teaching career. With other men, however, the outcome was not so fortunate. In 1899, Anderson submitted his resignation as missionary to Alaska. One reason was that during his two previous winters at Cheenik, his nasal catarrhal condition was aggravated by the rigorous climate. Another reason was that he wished to be free to carry on his mining operations in the summers without interruption. During the winter of 1899-1900, Hultberg also resigned. Illness was a factor, but the real reason was that when Hultberg became involved in a lawsuit with Lindblom, the Covenant executive committee sent him a telegram and letter, demanding that he desist from such litigation. Hultberg was angry at the committee for its attitude, and he was deeply annoyed because Anderson refused to testify in court for him. In the spring of 1902 Dr. C. W. Johnson of the Home of Mercy submitted his resignation as head physician and surgeon, and at the same time Dr. B. M. Linnell and Dr. C. H. Parkes also resigned. The reason for these resignations is not entirely clear, but it is certain that Dr. Johnson was in sharp disagreement with some of the Covenant trustees on such matters as Anderson's claims, No. 9 Above, and plans for a hospital. The resignation of these men hurt the Covenant's missionary and charitable enterprises, but the hardest blow of all was the resignation of Nyvall as secretary of the Covenant in 1903. He had served faithfully since 1895, had done a masterful job in writing detailed, interesting, and accurate year-books, and had carried on a prolific correspondence with missionaries, pastors, and officials. Despite every effort to persuade him to change his mind, Nyvall refused to withdraw his resignation. The reason was that the Alaska troubles had become an increasing nightmare, particularly for Nyvall, who disagreed sharply with the Covenant executive committee for repudiating the release of 1901.[8]

No. 9 Above had further ramifications for North Park College. Because of Nyvall's testimony before the arbitration com-

[8] Ill health was also a cause. Then, too, Nyvall was considering a trip to Sweden in 1904, a plan which did not materialize because of the death of his father, C. J. Nyvall, on May 22, 1904.

mission, people began to criticize both him and the school. Some congregations refused to have him speak and extended their antipathy to the institution whose lengthened shadow he was. A widening rift developed between Nyvall and Högfeldt, especially because of caustic, unfair and insinuating articles which appeared in the columns of *Missions-Vännen*. This rift continued for approximately twenty years and accounted for many of the denunciations leveled at the school. Above all, the differences on the Alaska gold mine led directly to Nyvall's resignation in 1905 as president of North Park College.

Nyvall accepted the presidency of Walden College, a newly established school at McPherson, Kansas. This school became a reality when Anderson gave $25,000 to erect a building. Unfortunately, the tentacles of the golden octopus of Alaska reached out to ensnare this school also. Because of litigation initiated by Hultberg in the District Court of Dickinson County, Abilene, Kansas, and in the District Court of the United States for the District of Kansas, Topeka, Kansas, the funds of the new conference school became involved; the financial problem increased and school rapport disintegrated.[9] Nyvall resigned on January 3, 1908, and thereafter the school declined until 1912, when it was sold because of inability to meet current obligations, to reduce interest charges and to pay teachers' pitifully small salaries.[10]

In discussing the various ramifications of the Alaskan gold dispute, we need to notice some of the legal aspects of the litigation. The contest itself was regarded by some lawyers as one of the most significant, interesting, prolonged and complex cases on record. That it was significant is apparent in the

---

[9] On September 9, 1907, just two days after Hultberg had begun his suit at Topeka, Kansas, David Brunstrom as Acting President of the School Association of the Swedish Evangelical Mission Conference of Kansas was served with a chancery subpoena. A subpoena was issued for President Nyvall also, but he was in Sweden on a speaking tour.

There is considerable information on Walden College in the files of the *McPherson Daily Republican* and the *Kansas Missions-Tidning*, both located in the files of the Kansas State Historical Society at Topeka.

[10] Nyvall's letter of resignation is printed in the *McPherson Daily Republican*, January 4, 1908, p. 1.

numerous lawyers and judges involved—approximately fifty—
and in the amount of money involved — approximately
$400,000. That it was interesting is seen in the close watching
of the decisions handed down, and in the articles, speeches, and
discussions resulting from the issues. The five years' wrangling
(1899-1904), besides the fifteen years' legal disputings (1904-
1919), sufficiently attest to the prolonged character of the litigation. So far as the complexity of the case is concerned, we
may note that one of the lawyers observed that the bitterly-
contested litigation was fought every step along the way, on any
issue conceivable to a judicial mind.

Among the issues raised in the arbitration commission, in
the state courts, and in the federal courts, we may note the following points. (a) Was the arbitration agreement one of special or general submission? (b) Did the Covenant as a nonprofit corporation have the right to own and operate a gold
mine? (c) If it did, why did it not do so? (d) If it did not,
why did it open itself up to the charge of maintenance by
transferring its rights to Hultberg? (e) Was the claim of Hultberg founded on maintenance? (f) Since there was no formal
accounting, did the judgment of $232,200 and $26,000 constitute a fraud, so far as the award was concerned? (g) Was
parole evidence, based on oral admissions, admissible and
worthwhile? (h) Was the release valid or void? (i) Did the
signature of a secretary and president bind the corporation or
denomination? (j) Did Judge Smith err in deciding that he
should not go into the merits of the case unless the award on
its face was characterized by fraud? (k) Was there a fiduciary
or trustee relationship between Anderson and the Covenant?
(l) If so, was it an express one? (m) If not, was it an implied trust? (n) If so, was it a constructive or resulting type?
(o) Could Eskimos own mines? (p) Were mines freeholds?
(q) Was a grubstaking contract, or a bed-rock contract, valid?
(r) Could mines staked by power of attorney be defended in the
courts? (s) Was it imperative for an attorney who had been
subpoenaed to divulge information about his client or his
whereabouts? (t) Did state courts violate the fifth and fourteenth amendments to the constitution in depriving litigants of

the right to due process of law and in abridging the liberty of contract?[11]

Besides these legal issues, we need to note, as another ramification of No. 9 Above, the lawsuits that paralleled the *Hultberg vs. Anderson* cases. As early as 1899 at San Francisco, Hultberg brought suit against Lindblom for alleged violation of a grubstake contract. Hultberg was unable to prove any such contract, so far as the Nome region was concerned. He was deemed to be in the wrong both by Anderson, who refused to testify for him, and by the Covenant executive committee, whose secretary demanded that Hultberg desist from his suit.

As a consequence of Mellander's article, published on March 2, 1903, in the Covenant's official organ, the *Missionären*, charging Anderson with improper and immoral conduct toward Dora Adams, an Eskimo girl, Anderson filed suit on February 18, 1904, against the Covenant and its executive committee and asked for damages of $75,000. This suit continued in the Circuit Court of Cook County without a hearing of the issues until November 15, 1909, when it was dropped.

The third suit which constituted a direct branching out from the case of No. 9 Above was the filing of charges by William A. Gilmore against the Covenant. Gilmore was a lawyer from Seattle, Washington, who established with Charles B. McConnell a law firm in Nome. It seems that during the summer or fall of 1900, Gilmore was consulted by O. P. Anderson, the successor of P. H. Anderson at Cheenik. O. P. Anderson had obtained a power of attorney from the officials of the Covenant, and then had discussed with Gilmore the means of compelling P. H. Anderson to give up his proceeds from No. 9 Above. In the spring of 1901, Gilmore informed some of the members of the executive committee that he had a claim for twenty per

[11] My own answers to these questions are as follows: (a) Special submission, subject to legal restrictions; (b) yes; (c) because it had no mine; (d) a reluctance to start a lawsuit; (e) no, but suspiciously close; (f) no, but a formal accounting would have avoided trouble; (g) admissible and of doubtful value, since much hearsay evidence is based on rumor, gossip, or malice; (h) valid; (i) yes; (j) I think so, because of Judge Sanborn's statements; (k) no; (l) no; (m) probably not; (n) resulting type, if there was any trust at all; (o) yes; (p) yes; (q) yes; (r) yes; (s) theoretically, yes, practically, no; (t) they seem to have restricted the right to due process of law by refusing to go into the merits of the case.

cent of all that the Covenant received from P. H. Anderson. In August, 1901, the release was sent to P. H. Anderson, who thereupon sent $54,000 to the Covenant. Evidently Gilmore learned that Anderson had donated approximately $100,000 for various Covenant causes, since he made a demand for $25,000 on December 5, 1901, and began formal proceedings in January-February of 1902. The case lingered on until the spring of 1905, when it was revived. After further delay, the case was set for July 16, 1906, in the United States Circuit Court for the Northern District of Illinois, Eastern Division, and a jury was impaneled. When Gilmore sought to obtain a further delay on July 11, 1906, Judge Christian C. Kohlsaat denied the motion for a continuance. Thereupon, the attorney for the plaintiffs, Gilmore and McConnell, moved that the case be dismissed, and Judge Kohlsaat ordered the case dismissed at the cost of the plaintiffs. The sole claim which the plaintiffs could make was that they were entitled to $25,000 as attorneys' fees on the basis of a contract made with O. P. Anderson. Since they were unable to produce any written contract, and since Anderson denied making any written or verbal contract, it seems that the plaintiffs hoped for some out-of-court compromise settlement by exorbitant demands in court.[12]

One final ramification of the Alaskan gold litigation deserves a brief mention. This was a lawsuit instigated by the Good Hope Mining Company, an organization of Covenant officials and members, against John L. Hagelin. On June 1, 1898, Hagelin had signed a contract, wherein he promised to prospect for minerals—especially coal and gold—for the company, in return for which he was to receive $50 a month. Hagelin was fortunate in that he accompanied Brynteson and Hultberg in their first trip to Nome in August, 1898. After Hagelin had prospected further in the Council City area, he left for home, and arrived in Chicago in December, 1898. During the time he was returning home, Brynteson staked No. 3 Above on Anvil Creek by a power of attorney for Hagelin.

---

[12] *Förbundets Adertonde Årsmöte i Galesburg, Illinois, Rapport till För-samlingarna,* pp. 64 f.; see also the report for 1905, pp. 82 f., and for 1907, p. 24. *Abstract of Record,* pp. 256, 275, 276, 305, 306. The *Nome Nugget,* August 23, 1901, p. 3.

When Hagelin returned home, he settled with the Good Hope Mining Company by paying $10,000 in return for a quit claim deed to his mines.[13]

This was the background of the suit, *The Good Hope Mining Company vs. John L. Hagelin,* initiated on August 28, 1900. The mining company had learned that Hagelin was a richer man than he represented himself to be. Evidently, he had mentioned his claims in the Eldorado district near Council City, and had minimized their value. The company alleged further that he had not mentioned his claims around Nome, No. 4 on Rock Creek and No. 3 on Anvil Creek, the latter claim reputedly being worth $300,000 and producing daily about $2000. Thus, claimed the company, Hagelin had obtained his deed fraudulently by misrepresenting the facts. Therefore, the plaintiffs, on September 10, 1900, prayed for possession of the two Nome claims, requested an accounting, and petitioned for a receiver. Judge Noyes took the matter under advisement, and on September 19, appointed Harry C. Gordon as receiver for both properties.[14]

Conclusions

Three separate trips were made to Nome, in August, September, and October. On the first trip, there was prospecting on Anvil Creek but there was no staking. On the second trip, claims were staked up to No. 6 Above inclusive. There is some evidence that No. 8 and No. 9 were intended for the Eskimo boys but since No. 7 was not staked until October 18, and since no stakes were found on Nos. 7, 8, and 9, it seems fairly certain that there was no official staking of these three claims in September. Even if we assume that they were staked, they were illegal holdings, since there was no recording of the claims, there was no proper marking on the stakes, and the dimensions of the claims were too large.

---

13 *Abstract of Record,* pp. 256, 268, 269.

14 The Nome *Daily Chronicle,* August 29, 1900, p. 1, and September 11, 1900, p. 1; Nome *Daily News,* August 29, 1900, p. 1, and September 20, 1900, p. 1. The lawsuit was tried at Nome in The District Court for the Territory of Alaska, Second Division.

Therefore, when the third trip was undertaken in October, the prospectors began anew. This time No. 7 was staked by Dr. A. N. Kittilsen, No. 8 by G. W. Price, and No. 9 by Price for his brother R. L. Price. No one disputed the ownership of No. 7 and No. 8, even though the latter mine was the second richest on Anvil Creek, and even if it is admitted that originally it was intended for Constantine, one of the Eskimo boys. The real dispute involved No. 9.

Several points of view are possible on No. 9. One is that when P. H. Anderson purchased this claim for $20, he did so for his own benefit. This is essentially the view of Anderson as purchaser, of G. W. Price as seller, and of Dr. Kittilsen as eye-witness of the staking and of the drawing up of the quit-claim deed. Legally, there is no doubt that Anderson was the owner, and morally, the testimony of these first-hand eye-witnesses and on-the-spot participants is well-nigh conclusive.

A second possible view is that Anderson was a kind of co-owner with the Eskimo boys. Anderson freely admitted that he intended to help the boys, and Price testified that he understood that Anderson wanted No. 9 in order to benefit the Eskimos. Since the original stakers believed that Eskimos were aliens and ineligible to hold claims, it is conceivable that they believed that an understood co-ownership was the answer. If so, nevertheless, they did not ask for any written legal instrument to this effect and they never specified what proportion of the proceeds should belong to the boys and to Anderson. If we assume this view, as Brynteson, Lindblom, and Dr. Johnson occasionally seemed to do,[15] then we must admit that Anderson's title was legally and morally clear after 1902, when he settled the Eskimos' claims, filed in the United States District Court of Alaska, Second Division, by a payment of $57,000, of which $26,500 went to the Eskimos and the remainder to the lawyers in the case.

---

[15] Unfortunately, Brynteson's position is vague. He expressed himself in one way to some of the members of the executive committee. When he met with Anderson in a formal meeting, he agreed with Anderson's version of the acquisition of No. 9 Above. In his Deposition of October 15, 1900, he defended Anderson in the lawsuit, Comptois *vs.* Anderson (*Abstract of Record,* pp. 408-421). Dr. Johnson was strongly for Anderson, and Lindblom was mildly against him.

A third possible view is that Anderson was a trustee. According to some, he was a trustee for the Eskimo boys. Others held that he was a trustee for the Alaskan mission station at Cheenik. Still others believed that he was a trustee for the Covenant. It is possible to believe that the intention of the original stakers was to set up a trustee for the boys for the sake of avoiding legal objections to any direct ownership by the Eskimos. If so, we must admit that this trustee relation is based on intentions and not on written instruments. We must also admit that the Eskimos' claims were extinguished by their accepting the court settlement of 1902 and by their legal confession that they held no interest whatsoever in the mine.

The argument that the mission station in Alaska was the intended beneficiary is somewhat ambiguous. By the mission station it may be interpreted to mean the owners—the Covenant; or it may be meant Anderson and Hultberg, who directed the station; or the entire Alaskan work at Cheenik, Unalakleet, and Yakutat may be intended; or the station at Cheenik and the Eskimos jointly may be meant. This latter view was expressed by one of the arbitrators, who believed that since the mission station had helped to rear the boys, the Eskimos owed some of their benefits to the mission station. The counter-argument is that the aid to the boys was relatively small, that they attended school irregularly, and that they more than compensated for their schooling and occasional lodging by their work as reindeer herders for the Covenant's herd.

We are thus forced to assume that if Anderson was a trustee at all, the best of these views would be that he was a trustee for the Covenant. Tentatively accepting this conclusion, we are compelled to seek the nature and origins of such a trustee relationship. It was not an express trust, since no written instruments existed for such a fiduciary relationship. If it was an implied trust, it must have been of the constructive or resulting type. Petterson held to the former view, since he stated bluntly:

> My idea was Anderson was our man, and he should make reports for his work out there, either mission work or money affair or any other kind. On that account we made a claim. We did not send him out as a gold miner, but

149

sent him out as a missionary, but he took the time and
found the gold also. He took our time, and—well, whatever it is up in Alaska that belongs to the Mission—belongs to us.[16]

Expressed differently, Petterson and other members of the
Covenant believed that Anderson's trusteeship was a true in-
ference from the nature of his position. The constructive aspect
of the trust was implicit in the fiduciary relationship of any
missionary with his sponsoring organization.

If we assume that the trust was an implied one, of the resulting type, as arbitrator Gilbert did, then we must needs prove
that the Covenant supplied gratis the provisions which made the
expedition possible. This, however, is impossible to do. It was
proved that Brynteson and Price paid for their supplies, that
Kittilsen and Lindeberg possessed their own stock of provisions,
and that any supplies obtained in addition were purchased. It
can be alleged that the mission station's boat and tools were
used, but the answer to this allegation was that the prospectors
made an agreement to aid Anderson in the building of a school
house in return for the use of the tools and boat. It was claimed
by Hultberg, and intimated by Petterson, that a grubstake contract was involved, explicitly or implicitly. This was denied by
all the participants, and in the light of the fact that Hultberg
was not present in Alaska when the expedition set out, both in
September and in October, and that Hultberg was unable to
produce any written contract, we must conclude that a resulting
trust was nonexistent.

The conclusion, therefore, is that the legal basis for a trust
of any kind rested on weak supports. Nyvall expressed the
truth of the matter when he said that there was not enough
proof on the disputed points to commence a lawsuit against
Anderson.[17] But Petterson asserted: "We are satisfied in our
minds that the claim belonged to us from all the questions

---

[16] Supreme Court of Illinois, No. 3912. White Star Mining Company of
Illinois *vs.* Nels O. Hultberg, The Swedish Evangelical Mission Covenant of
America *et al., Reply for Appellant, White Star Mining Company of Illinois,
and Appellees, Claes W. Johnson and Peter H. Anderson, to Argument for
Appellees, Nels O. Hultberg and The Swedish Evangelical Mission Covenant
of America, in Reply to the Petition for Rehearing,* pp. 56, 68.

[17] Nyvall Manuscripts.

asked from people." Despite these differences of opinion, we may confidently assert that it is certain that there was no express trust. It is equally certain that there was no basis for an implied trust of the constructive type, arising from Anderson's position as a missionary. The only possible *legally valid* position is the one taken by Gilbert, who held that an implied resulting trust derived from the furnishing of supplies. But the participants were able to prove that their provisions were not furnished gratis, and that there was no evidence for or even talk of any grubstake arrangement. Therefore, from the legal standpoint, Anderson was the undisputed owner of No. 9 Above. This was the conclusion of Judge Walter H. Sanborn, of the United States Circuit Court of Appeals for the Eighth Circuit, who wrote in his opinion of January 7, 1918:

> In the face of these facts, the evidence that he [Anderson] held Claim No. 9 or the proceeds of it in trust for the Covenant in December, 1899, or in April, 1901, when the deeds were made [for Mrs. Anderson] and paid for, not only utterly fails to prove such a trust, but it is so weak as to be almost negligible.[18]

Though we are compelled to award the *legal* victory to Anderson, it does not follow that he won the moral or ethical victory. It is possible that the pioneer prospectors intended to aid the Eskimos and to stake No. 9 Above at least partly for the Covenant. If that is so, they may have changed their intentions, or they may have readily accepted the plan of Price to stake a mine for Anderson, with a tacit understanding that Anderson would aid the denomination and the mission station and the Eskimos. Anderson and Price, however, had an understanding that Price would stake a mine for Anderson in return for the favors he had received. Thus, there is room for honest difference of opinion here. The worst construction put upon Anderson's actions, of course, was that he intended to operate No. 9 Above as a trustee for the Covenant, but as the increasing value of the mine became apparent, he changed his mind and rationalized his legal ownership into complete personal possession.

18 247 Fed. 273.

Something may be said in conclusion about the deficiencies of the three main participants, Anderson, Hultberg, and the Covenant. Anderson certainly weakened his own position by his reprehensible moral conduct. Many people concluded, erroneously, that if he was culpable in one sphere, he was blamable in another. Some criticized him for eluding summons, removing himself from the jurisdictions of courts, and delaying justice. Such actions probably stemmed partly from his attorneys' advice, and partly from an understandable desire to elude the ever-pursuing Hultberg. Also, in the light of Anderson's oral admissions—which he too categorically denied— it may be said that he could have avoided criticism and rumors by giving more definite assurances in 1899 and 1900.

So far as Hultberg was concerned, it may be said that animosity, frustration, and jealousy are behind his litigious actions. The animosities felt toward Anderson, Blake, the Covenant, Hagelin, Lindblom, and Nyvall stem from his frustration and jealousy. Hultberg left Alaska just three weeks before the greatest gold discovery in Alaskan history. Hultberg felt that he was responsible for this discovery, and complained, rightly so we believe, that others reaped where he had sowed. Furthermore, he was defrauded of a goodly portion of his mine, No. 5 Above, by a sharp-dealing syndicate. When we consider that he had spent five years in Alaska, had suffered ill-health, had seen his child die at Cheenik, and had felt that he himself and his wife had been mistreated by Anderson, we can understand better Hultberg's attitudes, while admitting at the same time that he was aggressive, contentious, tactless, visionary, and quick to make promises that were difficult to keep.

The executive committee of the Covenant was somewhat responsible for the developments which arose out of the discovery of No. 9 Above. Up until 1901, it had not paid its missionaries in northern Alaska in cash but rather in goods. This made possible some confusion about which goods belonged to Hultberg and which to Anderson. Furthermore, the committee was unduly sensitive to influences exerted by the publication, *Missions-Vännen*, whose financial and editorial policies were guided by Petterson and Högfeldt. Likewise, the denomination was understandably influenced at times by the actions and recommendations of this newspaper, as well as by its own executive committee.

It is easy to find fault with the executive committee. Let it be said in defense of its members that they were conscientious, altruistic-minded men of genuine Christian ideals. Let it also be said that they were men of strong convictions. But men of strong convictions are likely to see things as black or white, are prone to jump to conclusions, and are impatient of distinctions, reservations, and compromises. Two of the leaders in the executive committee were especially of this type—Mellander and Petterson, and from these two men came decisions which unduly influenced the executive committee and therefore the entire denomination.

The gravest indictment against the executive committee, as well as the denomination, was its vacillating policy. In February of 1901, the executive committee rejected Anderson's offer of $54,000. Instead, it countered with a demand for $100,000 plus one-half of all the future net proceeds of No. 9 Above. When Anderson rejected this demand, the sub-committee feared it would lose the $54,000 originally offered. Thereupon, in April, it decided that it would "hereafter consider P. H. Anderson's proposition as a voluntary donation, and consequently regard the matter against him settled, with mutual confidence and mutual friendship." It instructed its secretary, Nyvall, to write to Anderson of this changed attitude, and he did so. But Anderson had become wary as a result of this experience, and asked for a release. While the subject of a release was being debated, the annual conference, meeting at Duluth in June, accepted the decisions of the executive committee and expressed its thanks to Anderson by standing up. On August 6, Anderson received his release, signed by the president and secretary of the Covenant.

When the release was returned because it implied that Anderson's donations were a result of a debt of $54,000, a second release was sent which stated that the Covenant, in consideration of the sum of One Dollar, had released and forever discharged

P. H. Anderson from all causes of action, suits, debts due, claims and demands whatsoever in law or equity.

With this decision the dispute should have ended. If the Covenant later discovered it had made a bad bargain, or even if it became convinced that rightfully the mine was Covenant property, it should have observed the terms of the release. Instead, it permitted its own missionary, K. J. Hendrickson, to bring suit in 1902 against Anderson in the United States District Court of Alaska. This lawsuit cost Anderson approximately $57,000. Then, influenced by the writings and speeches of Mellander, who confused legality and morality, the Covenant annual conference in 1903 assigned its rights to Hultberg. In 1903, the Covenant had no rights to assign. Faced with threats from Hultberg to sue Anderson, regardless of what the denomination did, the executive committee was "high-pressured" into making its decision, and the annual conference was kept in line by Mellander. The conference went further when it appointed a committee to consult with a lawyer in order to declare null and void the release of August 16, 1901. By these actions, and by an alteration in the minutes of the sub-committee—on Mellander's motion, the denomination exposed itself to the charges particularly emphasized by the opposition lawyers— that the Covenant defaulted on its own release, that it heaped financial burdens and moral obloquy upon Anderson, and that it failed to practice the precepts of Christ, that it was guilty of maintenance, and that it permitted itself to be pushed around by the litigious Mr. Hultberg.

In conclusion, something may be said about the courts and the costliness of resorting thereto. Much of the legal trouble stemmed from the arbitration commission. H. T. Gilbert's vote was the lone decision that caused the subsequent litigation. One lawyer later declared that Gilbert's decision was "political," and a judge of the United States Circuit Court of Appeals found that the legal basis for a trusteeship, as represented by Gilbert, was negligible.[19] The legal contentions among lawyers and judges

[19] The lawyer was Carl R. Chindblom, who worked on this case, and the judge was Walter H. Sanborn of the Eighth Circuit.

indicated that objective law was very much dependent on subjective interpretation. The refusal of the courts to pass upon the merits of the case led to arguments in the briefs, asserting that the fourteenth amendment had been violated, since the litigant had been deprived of his property without due process of law.

So far as the costliness of the litigation was concerned, no accurate answer is possible. In actual money, the costs for Anderson probably exceeded $100,000. If one includes court costs, printing bills, legal fees for approximately thirty lawyers, travel expenses for participants, the amount involved for both plaintiff and defendant may reach $150,000-$200,000. Out of a gross income of $500,000 from No. 9 Above, therefore, one must deduct the cost of litigation, the operating expenses of $175,000, and the donations made to the Covenant of approximately $100,000. The net income, thus, would seem to be $125,000.[20]

In addition to the monetary costs, we must include the intangible price paid. For presidents C. A. Bjork and E. G. Hjerpe, the litigation was a constant worry. For Nyvall, No. 9 Above meant endless work, resignation as secretary of the Covenant, misunderstanding, unjust public odium, family heartaches, ill health and resignation as president of North Park College. For Anderson and Hultberg, it meant an upset family life, loss of serenity of spirit, bitter public criticism, and loss of friends. For Mellander and Petterson, it meant disillusionment. For the Covenant at large, No. 9 Above resulted in headaches, divided loyalties, loss of respect, injury to the growth of her institutions, attitudes of suspicion and carping criticism. It also meant the loss of possible future donations.

---

[20] Legal fees in Alaska approximated $40,000-$50,000. The costs in the United States are estimated as $30,000 for attorneys and $20,000 for travel expenses, court costs, and printing. The arbitration commission cost Anderson about $10,000. In the final settlement, in 1920, the balance of $28,361.53, held by the receiver, really belonged to Anderson, but he agreed to give $15,000 to the Covenant and Hultberg (probably mostly to their lawyers), and $13,361.50 to his own attorney, John J. Healy. It is almost certain that the judgment of $26,000 plus 5% interest for three years and forty-five days ($4062.45), was paid from Anderson's money. Thus the cost would at least amount to $158,423.98. Hultberg probably spent $40,000-$50,000.

As we think back over the twenty years of strife, and consider the negative results of Hultberg's action, it seems that the case of No. 9 Above resembles the fable of the person who killed the goose that laid the golden eggs.

CHRONOLOGICAL SUMMARY OF NO. 9 ABOVE

1887, June 25	A. E. Karlson arrives at St. Michael, Alaska.
1893, June 30	Hultberg arrives at Golovnin Bay.
1897, August 12	P. H. Anderson arrives at Golovnin Bay.
1897, December 28	First trip to Nome by Blake and Hultberg.
1898, July	Brynteson, Lindblom and Lindeberg arrive in Alaska.
1898, July 31	Hultberg begins second trip to Nome. Brynteson's first trip.
1898, August 31	Hultberg leaves Golovnin Bay for the States.
1898, September 22	Brynteson, Lindeberg and Lindblom stake claims on Anvil Creek.
1898, October 18	No. 9 staked by G. W. Price for R. L. Price.
1898, November 17	No. 9 sold to P. H. Anderson. First deed.
1899, March 8	Second deed made out with notary's seal.
1899, June	First mining season begins on Anvil Creek.
1899, July	No. 9 jumped by Paddy Ryan.
1899, December	First discussion with Anderson about ownership of No. 9 Above.
1900, July 19	Judge A. H. Noyes arrives at Nome.
1900, July 23	Alexander McKenzie appointed receiver in Nome.
1901, February 7	Anderson promised gifts of $54,000.
1901, June 22	The conference at Duluth accepts Anderson's gifts.
1901, August 16	The second release signed by Bjork and Nyvall.
1902, May 5	Suit begun on behalf of Eskimo boys in the U. S. District Court of Alaska, Second Division.
1902, August 12	Suit terminated in favor of Anderson.
1903, January 3	Anderson transfers No. 9 to Dr. C. W. Johnson.
1903, March 2	Mellander publishes article against Anderson.
1903, March 3	Meeting of executive committee to discuss Hultberg's propositions.
1903, June 17	The Covenant transfers No. 9 to Hultberg.
1903, August 4	Hultberg serves notice of his ownership to Dr. Johnson.
1903, August 12	Submission of parties to arbitration.
1904, February 20	Arbitration commission meets.
1904, April 13	Award made in favor of Hultberg.
1904, April 16	Bill of Complaint filed in the Superior Court of Cook County.
1904, May 17	The case transferred to the Circuit Court of Cook County. Fifteen years of litigation follow.

DEED FOR MINING CLAIM

This Indenture, made this, the 17 day of November, A. D. 1898, between G. W. Price, of Golovin Bay, District of Alaska, party of the first part, and P. H. Anderson of Golovin Bay, District of Alaska, party of the second part.

That the said party of the first part being the true and lawful attorney of R. L. Price, of Sonora, Tuolumne County, California, to locate, sell, lease, bond, acquire, dispose of mines and mining claims in the District of Alaska, a copy of which is recorded in the Cape Nome Mining District. That the party of the first part, for and in consideration of the sum of twenty ($20) dollars, lawful money of the United States of America, to him in hand paid by the said party of the second part at or before the ensealing and delivery of these presents, the receipt whereof is hereby acknowledged, has remised, released and quit-claimed, and by these presents does remise, release and quit-claim unto the said party of the second part, and to his heirs and assigns forever, all claim to the following described mining claim:

Name of Claim: No. 9 Above.

Name of Locator: R. L. Price, by G. W. Price, attorney.

Name of District: Cape Nome.

Name of Stream: Anvil Creek.

The said claim was discovered on the 18th day of October, 1898, and located the same date.

(Description of claim by metes and bounds.)

Said claim being recorded in Cape Nome Mining District, and also all the estate, right, title, interest, property, possession, claim and demand whatsoever as well in law as in equity as the said party of the first part have in or to the above described claim and every part and parcel thereof.

To have and to hold all and singular the above mentioned and described claim unto the said party of the second part, his heirs and assigns forever, and the said party of the first part (G. W. Price), hereby expressly waives, releases and relinquishes unto the said party of the second part (P. H. Anderson), his heirs, executors, administrators and assigns, all right, claim, interest and benefit whatsoever in and to the above described claim, and each and every part thereof. This is given by or results from all the laws of this District of Alaska, pertaining to mining claims, and the said party of the first part for himself, his heirs, executors and administrators, does hereby covenant, promise and agree to and with the said party of the second part, his heirs and assigns, that he has not made, done, committed, executed and suffered any act or acts, thing or things whatsoever, whereby or by means whereof the above mentioned and described claim or any part or parcel thereof, now or at any time hereafter shall or may be impeached, charged or incumbered in any name or way whatsoever.

IN WITNESS WHEREOF, the said party of the first part hereunto set his hand and seal the day and year first above mentioned.

(Signed) G. W. PRICE.

Sealed and delivered in presence of:

A. N. KITTILSEN, M. D.,
ERIC O. LINDBLOM.

Filed for record 9 A. M., November 1, 1898. [December 11, 1898]

P. H. ANDERSON, Deputy Recorder.

Appendix III

BILL OF SALE

KNOW ALL MEN BY THESE PRESENTS, that R. L. Price, by his attorney in fact, G. W. Price, of Senora, Tuolumne County, California, party of the first part, for and in consideration of the sum of twenty dollars ($20), lawful money of the United States of America, to him in hand paid at or before the ensealing and delivery of these presents, by P. H. Anderson, of Golovin Bay, Alaska, party of the second part, the receipt whereof is hereby acknowledged, has granted, bargained, sold and delivered, and by these presents, does grant, bargain, sell and deliver unto the said party of the second part, all the following described personal property, to wit: Placer Mining Claim No. 9 Above on Anvil Creek in the Cape Nome District, Alaska, as recorded in the record books of said district.

To have and to hold the above described property, together with all the rights, privileges and appurtenances, thereunto appertaining or belonging unto the said party of the second part, his heirs, executors, administrators and assigns, to and for his own use and behoof forever. And the said party of the first part does vouch himself to be the true and lawful owner of the above described property and has full power, right and lawful authority to dispose of the same in the manner aforesaid and against any and all lawful claims and demands against the same he will forever warrant and defend.

IN WITNESS WHEREOF, I, R. L. Price, have hereunto set my hand and seal at Golovin Bay, in the District of Alaska, this 8th day of March, A. D. 1899.

This is a re-record of a certain deed for same property, dated November 17, 1898, and recorded in the records of said Cape Nome Mining District.

R. L. PRICE, (SEAL.)

By G. W. Price, his attorney in fact, by power of attorney, dated May 16, 1898, and recorded in the records of Cape Nome Mining District, October 21, 1898, Vol. I, page 150.

Signed and delivered in the presence of:

N. P. R. HATCH,
A. N. KITTILSEN, M. D.

Attached is a certificate of acknowledgment before L. B. Shephard, United States Commissioner, dated March 8, A. D. 1899, and a certificate of record, dated March 13, 1899. 12:25 P. M.

Also attached is a certificate of T. M. Reed, United States Commissioner, bearing date October 24, 1903, that the foregoing is a true and correct copy from the record, at Vol. 8, page 50 of the records of Cape Nome Precinct.

Appendix IV

STIPULATION OF 1903

In the Matter of the Arbitration
between Nels O. Hultberg
vs.
White Star Mining Company
and Others.

IT IS HEREBY STIPULATED AND AGREED, by and between NELS O. HULTBERG, THE WHITE STAR MINING COMPANY OF ILLINOIS, CLAES W. JOHNSON and such other parties to said arbitration as may sign this stipulation, that the arbitrators of this matter shall assume and consider as facts proved the following:

First. That Cape Nome is a mining district, in the District of Alaska, and that No. 9 Above Discovery is a placer mining claim located in Anvil Creek, in said District.

Second. That A. N. Kittilsen, M. D., was the Recorder for said Mining District during the month of October, 1898, and that the lands in said District are unsurveyed Government lands, containing mineral deposits.

Third. That on October 19, 1898, there was filed for record a location notice as of a placer mining claim for said No. 9 Above on Anvil Creek by R. L. Price, acting by G. W. Price, his attorney in fact, as locator, reciting that said claim was discovered on the 18th day of October, 1898, and located on the same date. That said location notice now appears of record on Vol. I, page 36, in the Recorder's office of said Mining District.

Fourth. That by two instruments of conveyance, appearing of record, respectively, in Vol. 2, at page 238, and in Vol. 8, page 50, said R. L. Price deeded said placer mining claim No. 9 Above, on Anvil Creek, and such interests as said R. L. Price had therein, to P. H. Anderson. That the date of the instrument in said Vol. 2 being November 17, 1898, and the date of record November 1, 1898.* The date of the instrument in Vol. 8 being March 8, 1899, and the date of the record thereof 12:25 p. m., March 13, 1899. The recited consideration in said deeds being in each $20.

Fifth. That subsequently, by an instrument dated May 28, 1902, and recorded June 16, 1902, in Vol. 106, page 198, said P. H. Anderson conveyed to the White Star Mining Company, a corporation then organized and existing under the laws of the State of California, all his right, title and interest in said placer mining claim, No. 9 Above, said instrument purporting on its face to convey title absolute of said placer mining claim to the said company, and reciting the consideration as ten ($10) dollars.

Sixth. That ever since said location by R. L. Price all necessary assessment work required under the mining claim laws has been done, or been caused to be done by said Peter H. Anderson for the years of 1899, 1900 and 1901, by the White Star Mining Company of California for the year 1902, and by the White Star Mining Company of Illinois for the year 1903. That proof of such assessment work as has been necessary has been duly filed for record.

* This is an error to ascribe the date of record as prior to the instrument itself. The correct date is either December 1 or December 11, 1898.

Seventh. That by its deed of conveyance, dated May 19, 1903, and recorded June 16, 1903, in Vol. 117, at page 491, said White Star Mining Company of California conveyed said placer mining claim to the White Star Mining Company, a duly organized and existing corporation under the laws of the State of Illinois.

It, however, is understood and agreed, that nothing herein contained is intended to exclude other competent evidence of the facts above mentioned, and it is expressly agreed that either of the parties participating in this arbitration may introduce in evidence the original of any of the above mentioned instruments, or properly and duly certified copies thereof, as they may desire.

Nothing herein contained is intended to preclude the parties hereto from establishing on the hearing in whom the title to said placer mining claim, or the possession or the right to the possession thereof, in 1898, or subsequently, vested, or the true ownership thereof, nor from proving any matter of agency, trust, estoppel, or equity superior to the legal title.

In the event that the documents above referred to are produced in evidence, full value, credit and effect should be given to such documents, and the recitals therein. In all cases certified copies of documents offered in evidence are admissible in like manner as the originals would be if produced.

NOME, August 14, 1903.

NELS O. HULTBERG.
CLAES W. JOHNSON.
WHITE STAR MINING COMPANY OF ILLINOIS,
by CLAES W. JOHNSON, President.

161

Appendix V

JUDGES MAKING DECISIONS ON No. 9 ABOVE

Francis E. Baker—Judge in the United States Circuit Court of Appeals for the Seventh Circuit, 1913.
Theodore Brentano—Judge in the Superior Court of Cook County, 1904.
Edward O. Brown—Judge in the Appellate Court of Illinois, First District, 1904.
J. C. Cartwright—Chief Justice, Supreme Court of Illinois, 1905.
Melville W. Fuller—Chief Justice, Supreme Court of the United States, 1907.
John Gibbons—Judge in the Circuit Court of Cook County, 1908.
R. L. King—Judge in the District Court of Dickinson County of the Eighth Judicial District, Kansas, 1913.
Christian C. Kohlsaat—Judge in the District Court of the United States for the Northern District of Illinois, Eastern Division, 1912.
Kenesaw M. Landis—Judge in the United States Circuit Court of Appeals for the Seventh Circuit, 1913.
Jeremiah Leaming—Judge in the Circuit Court of Cook County, 1904.
Alfred S. Moore—Judge in the United States District Court of Alaska, Second Division, 1902.
O. L. Moore—Judge in the District Court of Dickinson County of the Eighth Judicial District, Kansas, 1907.
Adelor J. Petit—Judge in the Supreme Court of Illinois, 1912.
John F. Philips—Judge in the District Court of the United States for the District of Kansas, 1908.
M. W. Pinckney—Judge in the Circuit Court of Cook County, 1920.
John C. Pollock—Judge in the District Court of the United States for the District of Kansas, 1916.
Walter H. Sanborn—Judge in the United States Circuit Court of Appeals for the Eighth Circuit, 1918.
William H. Seaman—Judge in the United States Circuit Court of Appeals for the Seventh Circuit, 1913.
Frederick A. Smith—Judge in the Circuit Court of Cook County, 1904.
Charles M. Walker—Judge in the Circuit Court of Cook County, 1908.

LAWYERS INVOLVED IN LITIGATION ON No. 9 ABOVE

Worth E. Caylor—Attorney for White Star Mining Company.
Carl R. Chindblom—Attorney for White Star Mining Company.
Axel Chytraus—Attorney for White Star Mining Company.
E. Allen Frost—Attorney for White Star Mining Company.
Charles H. Hamill—Attorney for White Star Mining Company.
John J. Healy—Attorney for White Star Mining Company.
G. W. Hurd—Attorney for Mrs. P. H. Anderson.
Walter H. Jacobs—Attorney for Nels O. Hultberg.
James Hamilton Lewis—Attorney for Nels O. Hultberg.
E. C. Little—Attorney for Nels O. Hultberg.
McCulloch and McCulloch—Attorneys for Merchants' Loan and Trust
    Company.
John D. Milliken—Attorney for garnishee defendants in Kansas.
Olaf E. Ray—Attorney for P. H. Anderson and for Dr. Claes W. Johnson.
David Ritchie—Attorney for Nels O. Hultberg.
C. E. Rugh—Attorney for Nels O. Hultberg.
Charles Blood Smith—Attorney for Mrs. P. H. Anderson.
S. S. Smith—Attorney for Mrs. P. H. Anderson.
Harris F. Williams—Attorney for the Covenant.
Winston, Payne, and Strawn—Attorneys for Nels O. Hultberg.

Appendix VII

THE ELEVEN COURTS WHICH HEARD ARGUMENTS
ON No. 9 ABOVE

1. The United States District Court of Alaska, Second Division. Nome, Alaska.
2. The Superior Court of Cook County. Chicago, Illinois.
3. The Circuit Court of Cook County. Chicago, Illinois.
4. The District Court of Dickinson County, Kansas. Abilene, Kansas.
5. The Appellate Court of Illinois, First District. Chicago, Illinois.
6. The Supreme Court of Illinois. Springfield, Illinois.
7. The Circuit Court of the United States, Northern District of Illinois, Eastern Division. Chicago, Illinois.
8. The United States Circuit Court of Appeals for the Seventh Circuit. Chicago, Illinois.
9. The District Court of the United States for the District of Kansas. First Division. Topeka, Kansas.
10. The United States Circuit Court of Appeals for the Eighth Circuit. St. Louis, Missouri.
11. The Supreme Court of the United States. Washington, D. C.

CHRONOLOGICAL SUMMARY OF LITIGATION

1904, January 21	Hultberg begins a suit for $500,000 damages against Anderson in the Circuit Court of Cook County (No. 247,848).
1904, February 18	Anderson begins a suit for $75,000 damages against the Covenant and its executive committee, in the Circuit Court of Cook County.
1904, April 13	Arbitration commission makes its award in favor of Hultberg.
1904, April 15	Hultberg files suit on the basis of the award of April 13, 1904, in the Circuit Court of Cook County (No. 250,666).
1904, April 16	White Star Mining Company initiates a lawsuit against Hultberg in the Superior Court of Cook County (No. 236,166).
1904, May 17	Cases No. 250,666 and 236,166 are combined into one suit in the Circuit Court of Cook County (No. 251,594).
1904, June 13	Judge Smith affirms the decision of the arbitration commission (Case No. 251,594).
1904, June 20	Hultberg initiates a suit of attachment in the District Court of Dickinson County, Abilene, Kansas (No. 4332).
1904, July 1	Hultberg and the Covenant file their creditor's bill. Injunction and receiver obtained (No. 253,151).
1904, July 29	Anderson appeals to the Appellate Court of Illinois (Nos. 11,860-61).
1904, October	White Star Mining Company (No. 251,594) appeals to the Supreme Court of Illinois (No. 3912).
1904, November 28	Judge Brown affirms the interlocutory order of July 1 granting a receiver and an injunction (Nos. 11,860-61).
1904, December 12	Petition for rehearing to the Appellate Court of Illinois denied (Nos. 11,860-61).
1905, May 16	Mrs. Anderson's demurrer sustained by the District Court of Dickinson County (No. 4332).
1905, October 24	Decree of affirmance rendered by the Supreme Court of Illinois in favor of Hultberg (No. 3912).
1905, December	Petition by White Star Mining Company for a rehearing granted (No. 3912).
1906, April 17	Supreme Court of Illinois again affirms decree of June 13, 1904 (No. 3912).
1906, June 13	Petition for rehearing of second affirmance denied by the Supreme Court of Illinois (No. 3912).
1906, June 22	Application by the White Star Mining Company to the Supreme Court of the United States for a writ of error (No. 647).
1907, January 31	Hultberg secures judgment for $264,708 from Judge Moore—Abilene, Kansas (No. 4332).
1907, February 9	Writs of error allowed by the Supreme Court of the United States (No. 647).
1907, April 29	Writs of error dismissed for want of jurisdiction (No. 647).

1907, May 27	Petition for rehearing on decision of April 29 denied (No. 647).
1907, July	Judgment of $26,000 plus interest paid by White Star Mining Company to Hultberg.
1907, September 7	Hultberg begins suit in the District Court of the United States for the District of Kansas, First Division (No. 8609).
1908, May 28	Judge Walker orders cross-bills of Anderson *et al.* to be stricken from files (No. 253,151).
1908, October 2	Judge Walker denies Anderson's appeal to the Supreme Court (No. 253,151).
1908, November 12	Mrs. Anderson's second appeal to the Appellate Court of Illinois dismissed (No. 14,710).
1908, November 23	Decree *pro confesso* entered against Mr. and Mrs. P. H. Anderson (No. 8609).
1908, November 30	Petition for rehearing denied by the Appellate Court of Illinois (No. 14,710).
1909, January 19	The decree of November 23, 1908, vacated, so far as Mrs. Anderson was concerned (No. 8609).
1909, July 28	Praecipe filed to have the record sent to the Supreme Court of Illinois (Case No. 7712).
1910, June 21	Anderson files a bill of equity in the District Court of the United States, Northern District of Illinois, Eastern Division (No. 30,047).
1910, November 9	Case dismissed (No. 30,047) by Judge Kohlsaat of the District Court of the United States (No. 30,047).
1911, November 6	William Needles appointed special examiner by Judge Pollock (No. 8609).
1911, December 21	Decision rendered wherein the White Star Mining Company loses its appeal (No. 253,151) a second time in the Supreme Court of Illinois (No. 7712).
1912, February 7	The Supreme Court of Illinois denies a petition for rehearing (No. 7712).
1912, August 15	Hultberg petitions for a rule in the District Court of the United States, Northern District of Illinois, Eastern Division, to compel Attorney Chytraus to testify before special examiner Needles (No. 30,954).
1912, September 9	Mrs. Anderson successful in collecting costs from Hultberg—Abilene, Kansas (No. 4332).
1912, October 22	Hultberg's suit in the District Court of the United States dismissed at his cost (No. 30,954).
1912, October 31	Anderson appeals from the decision of November 9, 1910, to the Supreme Court of the United States (No. 374).
1912, November 17	William Needles, special examiner, dies (No. 8609).
1912, December 26	John E. McFadden appointed as special examiner (No. 8609).
1913, February	Hultberg appeals his case against Chytraus to the United States Circuit Court of Appeals for the Seventh Circuit (No. 1970).
1913, October 2	Hultberg's suit of attachment in Abilene, Kansas, dismissed for want of prosecution (No. 4332).
1913, November 21	Hultberg's appeal dismissed by the United States Circuit Court of Appeals for the Seventh Circuit (No. 1970).
1914, November 30	The Supreme Court of the United States affirms the order of dismissal of November 9, 1910 (No. 374).

1915, February 23	The Supreme Court of the United States dismisses the writ of error sought by the White Star Mining Company (No. 864).
1916, May 20	The District Court of the United States for the District of Kansas renders its decree in favor of Hultberg (No. 8609).
1916, June 26	Mrs. Anderson appeals the decision of May 20, 1916, to the United States Circuit Court of Appeals for the Eighth Circuit (No. 4837).
1918, January 7	All the previous court decisions reversed by Judge Sanborn of the United States Circuit Court of Appeals for the Eighth Circuit (No. 4837).
1918, September 2	United States Circuit Court of Appeals denies Hultberg's plea for a rehearing (No. 4837).
1918, December 16	United States Supreme Court denies Hultberg's plea for a writ of certiorari (No. 749).
1919, March 3	United States Supreme Court denies Hultberg's plea for a rehearing (No. 749).
1920, February 4	Judge Pinckney dismisses Hultberg's bill of complaint without costs (No. 253,151).
1920, February 20	Final order of the Circuit Court of Cook County dismissing the case (No. 253,151).

SELECT BIBLIOGRAPHY

MANUSCRIPTS

Alaska. The Alaska Historical Library and Museum. Juneau.
    Customs Records and Correspondence.
    Court Docket of Municipal Judge Alonzo Rawson.
Courts. County and State Court Original Records in Offices of Clerks of the
    Courts.
    Appellate Court of Illinois. No. 11,860, No. 11,861.
    Circuit Court of Cook County. No. 247,848, No. 250,666, No. 251,594,
        No. 253,151.
    District Court of Dickinson County, Abilene, Kansas. No. 4332.
    Superior Court of Cook County. No. 236,166.
    Supreme Court of Illinois. No. 3912, No. 7712.
        Court Docket Books
        Manuscript Record (2667 pages—best source)
Courts. Federal Court Original Records in Offices of Clerks of the Courts.
    (These records are mostly dockets, motions, testimony, and exhibits).
    The District Court for the Territory of Alaska, First Division. Juneau.
        No. 1006.
        Appointment Book.
        Court Journal No. 8.
    The District Court for the Territory of Alaska, Second Division. Nome.
        No. 8.
    The District Court of the United States for the Northern District of
        Illinois, Eastern Division, Chicago, Illinois. No. 30,047, No. 30,954.
    The District Court of the United States for the District of Kansas,
        First Division. Topeka, Kansas. No. 8609.
    The United States Circuit Court of Appeals for the Seventh Circuit.
        Chicago, Illinois. No. 1970.
    The United States Circuit Court of Appeals for the Eighth Circuit.
        St. Louis, Missouri. No. 4837.
    The United States Circuit Court of Appeals for the Ninth Circuit. San
        Francisco, California. No. 632, No. 634, No. 636, No. 701, No. 702,
        No. 703, No. 744.
    The Supreme Court of the United States. Washington, D. C. No. 374,
        No. 647, No. 749, No. 864.
Covenant Archives, Chicago, Illinois.
    Correspondence.
    E. G. Hjerpe Manuscripts.
    Mellander Manuscripts.
    Minutes of Special Sessions at Annual Conferences.
    Minutes of the Covenant Executive Committee.
    Minutes of the Sub-Committee of the Covenant Executive Committee.
    Nyvall Manuscripts.
Interview Material.
    P. H. Anderson, Carl R. Chindblom, S. G. Cronstedt, J. J. Healy, D.
        Nyvall, and W. Marshall.
National Archives, Washington, D. C.
    Departments of Interior, Justice, Legislature, and War.
Newberry Library, Chicago, Illinois.
    Manuscript of William Douglas Johns on Alaska.
North Dakota Historical Society, Bismarck, N. D.
    Alexander McKenzie Papers.
    Pinkerton Detective Agency Reports.
Presbyterian Historical Society; Philadelphia, Pennsylvania.
    Sheldon Jackson Correspondence, Volumes XVIII, XIX, XX.
Wickersham Manuscripts.
    These papers of Judge James Wickersham are in Juneau, Alaska, at the
        home of Mrs. James Wickersham. The diaries and letters are the
        most significant items.

ARTICLES

Carlson, Leland H. "The Discovery of Gold at Nome, Alaska," *The Pacific Historical Review,* September, 1946.
Carlson, Leland H. "The First Mining Season at Nome, Alaska—1899," *The Pacific Historical Review,* May, 1947.
Carlson, Leland H. "Nome: From Mining Camp to Civilized Community," *Pacific Northwest Quarterly,* July, 1947.
Carlson, Leland H. "The Scandinavians and the Great Alaskan Gold Rush," American Swedish Historical Foundation, *Year Book, 1948.* Philadelphia, 1948.
Castle, N. H. "A Short History of Council and Cheenik," *The Alaska Pioneer,* Vol. I, No. 1 (June, 1912).
Cowden, Fred R. "Cape Nome Mining District." *The Alaska Pioneer,* June 13, 1913.
Fitch, George Hamlin. "The New Gold-Camp under the Arctic Circle," *Harper's Weekly,* XLIII (December 2, 1899).
Hoffman, Hal. "Cape Nome," *Alaskan Magazine,* September, 1900.
"Latest News from Nome," *Alaskan Magazine,* September, 1900.
Morrow, William W. "The Spoilers," *California Law Review,* Vol. IV, No. 2 (January, 1916).
Whittlesey, W. H. "Wonderful Cape Nome," *Alaskan Magazine,* May, 1900.

BOOKS AND PAMPHLETS

Anderson, Theodor. *Svenska Missionsförbundet, dess uppkomst och femtio-åriga verksamhet.* Stockholm, 1928.
Beach, Rex. *Personal Exposures.* New York, 1940.
Beach, Rex. *The Spoilers.* New York, 1906.
Carlson, Leland H. *A History of North Park College.* Chicago, 1941.
Carpenter, Herman. *Three Years in Alaska.* Philadelphia, 1901.
The Case of Judge Arthur H. Noyes of Nome, Alaska. [Washington, D. C., 1901-02].
Colby, Merle. *A Guide to Alaska, Last American Frontier.* New York, 1939.
Curtin, Walter R. *Yukon Voyage, Unofficial Log of the Steamer Yukoner.* Caldwell, Idaho, 1938.
Dunham, Sam C. *The Goldsmith of Nome and Other Verse.* Washington, D. C., 1901.
Dunham, Sam C. *The Men Who Blaze the Trail and Other Poems.* New York, 1913.
Evangelical Mission Covenant Church of America. *Year Books,* 1885-1920. 37 vols. Cited under Swedish title. See under "Svenska."
Fitz, Frances Ella. *Lady Sourdough.* New York, 1941.
French, L. H. *Nome Nuggets, Some of the Experiences of a Party of Gold Seekers in Northwestern Alaska in 1900.* New York, 1901.
Grinnell, Joseph. *Gold Hunting in Alaska.* Ed. Elizabeth Grinnell. Elgin, Illinois, 1901.
Harrison, E. S. *Nome and Seward Peninsula.* Seattle, 1905.
Höijer, Arvid och Georg af Forselles. *Svenska Greven av Alaska. Guld-grävarliv i Nome, Candle, och Fairbanks.* Stockholm, 1934.
Johnshoy, Joseph W. *Apaurak in Alaska.* Philadelphia, 1944.
McElwaine, Eugene. *The Truth About Alaska ,the Golden Land of the Midnight Sun.* Chicago, 1901.
McKee, Lanier. *The Land of Nome. A Narrative Sketch of the Rush to Our Behring Sea Gold-fields, the Country, Its Mines and Its People, and the History of a Great Conspiracy, 1900-1901.* New York, 1902.
Morrell, W. P. *The Gold Rushes.* New York, 1941.
North American Transportation and Trading Company. *Alaska and the Gold Fields of Nome, Golovin Bay, Forty Mile, the Klondike, and Other Districts.* [Seattle], 1900.
Nyvall, David. *Alaska Förr och Nu.* Chicago, 1897.
Peterson, Nils and Lindgren, S. O. *Förbundets Komite och P. H. Anderson.*
Robinette, A. M. *Facts about Cape Nome and Its Golden Sands.* [Seattle], 1900.

Rydell, Carl. *Adventures of Carl Rydell, the Autobiography of a Seafaring Man.* Ed. Elmer Green. London, 1924.
Sullivan, May K. *A Woman Who Went to Alaska.* Boston, 1902.
Svenska Evangeliska Missions-Förbundet i Amerika. *Förbundets Arsberättelse. Rapport till Församlingarna.* 37 vols. Chicago, 1885-1920.
Trout, Peter. *My Experiences at Cape Nome, Alaska.* Seattle, 1899.
Tuttle, C. R. *The Golden North.* Chicago, 1897.
Underwood, John J. *Alaska, an Empire in the Making.* New York, 1915.
Wickersham, James. *A Bibliography of Alaskan Literature, 1724-1924.* Cordova, 1927.
Wirt, Loyal L. *Alaskan Adventures.* New York, 1937.

GOVERNMENT PUBLICATIONS

Baker, Marcus. *Geographic Dictionary of Alaska.* United States Geological Survey. Bulletin No. 187, Series F., Geography 27. 57th Congress, 1st session (serial 4366). House Document No. 469. Washington, D. C., 1901.
Blake, H. L. "History of the Discovery of Gold at Cape Nome," 56th Congress, 1st session (serial 3878). Senate Document No. 441. Washington, D. C., 1900.
Brady, John G. "Report of the Governor of Alaska," *Annual Reports of the Department of the Interior—Miscellaneous Reports.* 55th Congress, 2nd session (serial 3642). House Document No. 5. Washington, D. C., 1898.
Brooks, Alfred H. *et al. Reconnaissances in the Cape Nome and Norton Bay Regions, Alaska, in 1900.* 56th Congress, 2nd session (serial 4198). House Document No. 547. Washington, D. C., 1901.
Brooks, Alfred H. *et al. Report on Progress of Investigation of Mineral Resources of Alaska in 1906.* United States Geological Survey. Bulletin No. 314. Washington, D. C., 1907.
Collier, Arthur J., Hess, Frank L., Smith, Philip S., Brooks, Alfred H. *Gold Placers of Parts of Seward Peninsula, Alaska, Including Nome, Council, Kougarok, Port Clarence, and Goodhope Precincts.* United States Geological Survey, Bulletin 328. Washington, D. C., 1908.
Dunham, Sam C. "The Yukon and Nome Gold Regions," *Bulletin of the Department of Labor,* V (July). Washington, 1900. See also Volume III, No. 16 (May, 1898) and No. 19 (November, 1898).
Hansbrough, H. C. "Alien Mining Locations in Alaska—the Scandinavian Segregated from the Laplander," *Congressional Record,* April 30, 1900.
Jackson, Sheldon. *Report on Introduction of Domestic Reindeer into Alaska.* 55th Congress, 2nd session (serial 3590), Senate Document No. 30. Washington, D. C., 1898. Of the sixteen reports, issued 1891-1906, all except the first report were issued as U. S. Senate documents, and are listed in James Wickersham's *Bibliography.*
Schrader, Frank C., and Brooks, Alfred H. *Preliminary Report in the Cape Nome Gold Region, Alaska, with Map and Illustrations.* 56th Congress, 1st session (serial 3867). Senate Document No. 236. Washington, D. C., 1900.
United States, Department of the Interior. *Circular from the General Land Office Showing the Manner of Proceeding to Obtain Title to Public Lands under the Homestead, Desert Land, and Other Lands.* Washington, D. C., 1899.
United States, Department of the Interior. *Public Land Statutes of the United States.* Ed. Daniel M. Greene. Washington, D. C., 1931.
United States, House of Representatives. 55th Congress, 3rd session (serial 3874). House Document No. 47. Washington, D. C., 1898.
United States, House of Representatives. 56th Congress, 2nd session (serial 4072). House Document No. 2. Washington, D. C., 1901.
United States, Senate. *Congressional Record, Senate.* Especially for years 1897-1902.
United States, Senate. 55th Congress, 2nd session. Senate Document No. 30. Washington, D. C., 1899.
United States, Senate. 56th Congress, 1st session (serial 3868). Senate Document No. 72. Washington, D. C., 1900.

United States, Senate. 56th Congress, 1st session (serial 3868). Senate Document No. 72. Washington, D. C., 1900.
United States, Senate. 56th Congress, 2nd session (serial 4042). Senate Document No. 196, Vol. 14. Washington, D. C., 1901.
United States, Senate. 56th Congress, 2nd session (serial 4067). Senate Report No. 2414. Washington, D. C., 1901.
United States, War Department. *Annual Report of the War Departemnt for the Fiscal Year Ended June 30, 1899; Report of the Major-General Commanding the Army, Part I.* Washington, D. C., 1899.
Wines, Arthur Frederick. "Cape Nome Mining Region." 56th Congress, 1st session (serial 3875). Senate Document No. 357. Washington, D. C., 1900.

NEWSPAPERS

Abilene *Weekly Chronicle* (Kansas).
Aurora Borealis. (A typescript "newspaper," St. Michael).
Grand Forks *Evening Times* (North Dakota).
Grand Forks *Herald* (North Dakota).
McPherson *Daily Republican* (Kansas).
Missionären (Chicago).
Missions-Vännen (Chicago).
Kansas Missions-Tidning (Lindsborg).
Nome *Daily Chronicle.*
Nome *Daily News.*
Nome *Gold Digger.*
Nome *Nugget.*
San Francisco *Call.*
San Francisco *Chronicle.*
Yukon Press (Circle, Alaska).

PRINTED LEGAL RECORDS

Appellate Court of Illinois, First District, No. 11,860, No. 11,861. P. H. Anderson *vs.* Nels O. Hultberg.
  Brief and Argument for Appellees.
  Brief for Appellants.
Cases. *Alaska Federal Reports.* 1 *Al. Fed.* 663; 1 *Al. Fed.* 693.
Cases. *Illinois Reports.* 220 Ill. 578; 252 Ill. 607.
Cases. *Illinois Appellate Reports.* 117 Ill. App. 231; 144 Ill. App. 529.
Cases. *Federal Reporter.* 106 Fed. 775; 108 Fed. 985; 108 Fed. 988; 109 Fed. 710; 109 Fed. 971; 109 Fed. 975; 109 Fed. 1061; 111 Fed. 988; 121 Fed. 209; 121 Fed. 213; 121 Fed. 221; 146 Fed. 467; 170 Fed. 657; 203 Fed. 855; 214 Fed. 349; 247 Fed. 273.
Cases. *United States Reports.* 179 U. S. 686; 180 U. S. 536; 205 U. S. 541; 235 U. S. 692; 238 U. S. 692; 248 U. S. 581.
The District Court of the United States, District of Kansas, First Division. No. 8609. Nels O. Hultberg *vs.* P. H. Anderson.
  Bill in Equity.
The District Court of the United States, Northern District of Illinois, Eastern Division. No. 30,047.
  Bill in Equity.
  Exhibits.
Supreme Court of Illinois, No. 3912. White Star Mining Company of Illinois *vs.* Nels O. Hultberg *et al.*
  Abstract of Record.
  Appendix to Petition for Rehearing.
  Argument for Appellees.
  Brief and Arguments for Appellant.
  Petition for Leave to File Additional Petition for Rehearing.
  Petition for Rehearing by White Star Mining Company.
  Petition for Rehearing on Opinion.
  Reply for Appellant.
  Statement of the Case. Opinion of Judge Frederick A. Smith. Opinion of Arbitrator Hiram T. Gilbert.

171

Supreme Court of Illinois, No. 7712. Nels O. Hultberg *vs.* P. H. Anderson.
> *Brief and Arguments for Defendants in Error.*
> *Brief and Arguments for Plaintiffs in Error.*
> *Reply for Plaintiffs in Error.*

The Supreme Court of the United States, No. 647. C. W. Johnson *vs.* N. O. Hultberg.
> *Transcript of Record.*

The Supreme Court of the United States, No. 374. P. H. Anderson *vs.* The Swedish Evangelical Mission Covenant of America.
> *Brief for Appellants.*
> No. 64. *Transcripts of Records and File Copies of Briefs, 1914.* Vol. XIX, Cases No. 64-66.
> No. 749. *Ibid.* Vol. CVI, Cases No. 717-754.
> No. 412. *Ibid.* Vol. LIV, Cases No. 405-414.
> No. 462. *Ibid.* Vol. XLIII, Cases No. 446-479.

The United States Circuit Court of Appeals for the Eighth Circuit. No. 4837. Friedeborg A. Anderson *vs.* Nels O. Hultberg.
> *Brief and Argument for Appellee.*
> *Petition for Rehearing by Appellee.*
> *Transcript of Record.*

United States Circuit Court of Appeals for the Ninth Circuit. No. 632. P. H. Anderson, Appellant, *vs.* O. Jose Comptois, Appellee.
> *In the Matter of the Alleged Contempt of Dudley Dubose in Having It is Said, Advised O. Jose Comptois the Appellee, to Disobey and Refuse to Comply with the Terms of the Writ of Supersedeas Duly Issued Herein.* [1901].

United States Circuit Court of Appeals for the Ninth Circuit.
> *Records in the Matter of the Contempt Case of Alexander McKenzie.* 3 vols. [1901].
> *Records in the Matter of Contempt Cases in re. A. H. Noyes.* 11 vols. [1901].
> (The original records are in San Francisco, in the office of the clerk of the Court. There are three printed sets, at the Library of Congress, at the National Archives, and at the Alaska Historical Library and Museum).

INDEX

INDEX

177

Watterson, John, 15

White Star Mining Company of California, 50, 51, 56, 57, 70, 73, 91, 95

White Star Mining Company of Illinois, 57, 70, 73, 78, 99, 100, 110, 111, 114-117, 124, 126-128

Wickersham, James, 21

Williams, Harris F., 78, 109, 130

Wilson, C. G., 116

Youngberg, C., 45

Youngquist, C. August, 6, 17-19, 43, 58, 68, 69, 72, 83, 84, 94

Zeisler, Sigmund, 117